I'm Screaming
Can You Hear Me?
Volume I

Dr. M. H. Hancock

Kingdom Builders Publications LLC

I'm Screaming, Can You Hear Me?
Copyright © 2016 by Dr. M Hancock
Kingdom Builders Publications

All rights reserved. No part of this book may be reproduced or transmitted in any form or by any means without written permission from the author.

ISBN:
Paperback: 978-0-692-73452-0
Library of Congress Control Number 2016944126
Cover Designer – LoMar Designs
Photographer – "Just Pose" L H Photography

Editors:
Kingdom Builders Publications Editorial Staff
Angela Williams

Printed in USA
Go to this website for bookings and ordering:
www.kingdombuilderspublications.com

All Holy Scriptures are taken from the King James Version of the Bible unless otherwise stated.

This Book Belongs to

DEDICATION

I dedicate this book to the body of Christ who desire to reach destiny; to those who have realized the Word of God; knowing we will overcome every obstacle faced in our lives; We are truly rich, because the blessings of the Lord are running us over and blessing us. Deuteronomy 28:2 says: And all these blessings shall come on thee, and overtake thee, if thou shalt hearken unto the voice of the Lord thy God. Let us not forget those things God has assigned to our hands to do because all of us have different talents to help build the kingdom of God (Matthew 25:15). This book is dedicated to those who feel like there is no hope for their situation. BUT GOD can and will do just what He said in His Word. His Word says His thoughts are good and not evil toward us (Jeremiah 33:11). This book is dedicated to those who feel like they cannot bounce back from something they did or someone did to them. Again, BUT GOD makes the difference in every situation and if He brought me back to my place in Him then I know He CAN and WILL do the same thing for you.

CONTENTS

	Dedication	iv
	Acknowledgments	vi
1	State of Being	7
2	Present State	14
3	Where Are We?	28
4	The Chronicle of our Cries	51
	About the Author	128
	References	129

ACKNOWLEDGMENTS

I thank God for my man of God, Antoine M. Hancock. I am truly blessed because he covers me and knows who he is in God; I am free to do what God tells to me to do. One thing I'm especially thankful for is my family (the Harrisons, Hancock's, Barnes, Lanes, Lowe's, Haddads, Gills and Williams) and friends who encourage me to continue doing what has been assigned me. I acknowledge the angels in our lives; our children, Alexus, Alyah, and Myah Hancock. Antoine and I have obtained favor of the Lord to be blessed with kingdom kids.

Additionally, to my church family, I thank God for each of you and your families. I believe we are all here to reach people. God bless you in your journey to discover who you are, your calling in God; and how are to achieve those goals with God.

Thank God for my publishing company and Mrs. Louise Smith. I thank God for being obedient and calling when I did. I know I am in very capable hands with Kingdom Builders Publications Company.

STATE OF BEING
Chapter One

MIND SET

I AM SCREAMING BECAUSE I cannot get my mind to conform to the Word of God.

Romans 12:2 *And be not conformed to this world: but be ye transformed by the renewing of your mind, that ye may prove what is that good, and acceptable, and perfect will of God.*

Our mindset is powerful because whatever 'WE' believe or perceive to be, it is. It does not matter if the situation is true or not, it becomes true because our mind tells us it is. When we set our mind on anything, there is nothing we cannot do. The same is when we believe something true or false, with evidence or without. It's now true because our will, intelligence or imagination tells us it is. Most times, we operate from the carnal perspective, so the God Spirit doesn't stand a chance. However, accepting Christ, we operate more from our Spiritual beings, and less in our flesh when dealing with the issues of life that effect our very being.

We have to ensure our Spiritual life is based on the Word of God because our children's lives from a mental, physical, Spiritual, and psychological

standpoint depends on it. If we don't train them up in the Word of God, they won't know what to do in crisis situations. The Word declares, ...*those who hunger and thirst for righteousness, they will be filled.*
St. Matthew 5: 6.

Additionally, we are not the only influences in our children's lives. School is a huge part of their makeup, media outlets to include: television and music are a big part of their lives. Sometimes as parents, we may feel the need to be our children's friends, but God has not called us to be their friends. Very few of our children understand Spiritual things and are unable to operate in the Spiritual world. We have to understand the impact we will have on our children's success in the natural and Spiritual worlds. Below are additional Scriptures for reading.

ADDITIONAL SCRIPTURES
Proverbs 3:5-6
St. Luke 12:29
Romans 12:2
II Timothy 1:7
Isaiah 26:3
Romans 8:27
Colossians 3:2

One thing can change the way we look at life is our will. This is when we want something to be so badly, regardless of the opposition from others, it taints the PERCEPTION in our FINITE mind. The Father sometimes has to step in and allow things to happen so He can help us re-focus.

We experience various things, and we ask the famous and daunting question, "Lord why me?" We, at that point, forget life happens as a result of the choices we make, good or bad. There is nothing or anyone that should occupy our inner most being, but the Father. The Word of God declares He is a jealous God and will not share His glory with anyone or anything.

ADDITIONAL SCRIPTURES
Exodus 34:14
Exodus 20:2
John 20:30-31
I John 3:20

It would be nice when situations happen out of our control or circumstances we don't like; that at the blink of an eye, they would dissolve, but it doesn't happen like that. Because of what is going on, we feel the screams surfacing in the realms of the natural and the Spirit. Well, the same thing happens in our Spirit as we make decisions opposite to what God's will is for our lives. Our soul begins to scream for help, guidance, revival, or restoration to the place God created for us.

Our soul becomes restless and it screams because we are not in the place where our Father is calling or has showed us through the Spirit.

Let's take a look at the game of chess. It's strategy helps one understand the position on how to beat his opponent. The players in the game of chess are the king, pawn, and knights. They are strategically positioned to constantly protect the "queen" which is the most valuably powerful but the weakest because of the king's limited moves in the chess game. The queen represents each person's destiny.

The ultimate goal of the enemy is to bring destruction and take our destiny by getting us out of right fellowship with the Father in Heaven. Each of us uses the strategies in the Word of God to protect our destiny (queen) such as prayer, praise, worship and the Word of God. As we get in the Word and apply the Word to our situations, we put the devil and his demons to flight in our lives.

The great news is the angels that are assigned to us, protect us, fight for us, and rage in battle for us. The Scripture tells us *We have overcome by the blood of the lamb and the words of our testimony*, but we have to believe what it says and operate on its authority for the Word to work for us.

So many of us allow the enemy to play the game of chess with our lives. Why and how you ask? Well, let me ask: Are you walking in the promises of God in every area of your life? Do you feel like you are on your way to receive all the things the Word of God has declared about your life? For most of us, the answer to these questions are emphatically no. The reasons we cannot answer in the affirmative is because we allow the distractions of the world, fear, intimidation, past mistakes, self and the enemy to place our destiny in 'check-mate.' In the game of chess, you say check mate when the queen is about to be taken, and the analogy for the 'queen' is our *destiny*. Moreover, before we allow the Lord to take control, we lose control because of our present circumstances or situation.

Psalm 103:20 says: *Bless the Lord, ye his angels that excel in strength, that do his commandments, hearkening unto the voice of his word.*

When any piece of a person's life is unguarded, he is open for assigned demons to attack, leaving that person's destiny dangerously vulnerable. In the game of chess, the more pieces taken, the more the opponent is stripped of power to protect his queen *destiny*. If our destiny / *queen* can't be protected, our destiny will be hindered and in some instances ultimately destroyed. GAME OVER!

Please understand the enemy only has the power YOU give him. The Bible teaches *death and life is in the power of our tongue*. So what we speak is either in favor or against the Word of God. Sometimes we destroy things in our lives based on our words and actions. If we speak negative things, negative results occur. We are quick to blame the enemy for decisions we make. That's right, we destroy our destiny with our own words. We help the enemy destroy our lives when we speak negative things. I believe the enemy distracts us from the purpose of God and the love of God because he was once part of Heaven.

Later in life, we can't seem to reach our destiny, thus begin screaming in our actions or the lack of actions. Choosing the wrong things to do and hanging around the wrong crowd dulls the senses, our directions, and decisions.

I want to be clear that the devil is not the only one who can destroy our destiny; we have that power also. We have to know the power God gave us as joint-heirs with Christ.

2 Corinthians 10:3-5 says: *For though we walk in the flesh, we do not war after the flesh: For the weapons of our warfare are not carnal, but mighty through God to the pulling down of strongholds; Casting down imaginations, and every high thing that exalteth itself against the knowledge of God, and bringing into captivity every thought to the obedience of Christ;*

We have to apply the Word of God at all times and in every situation.

I'm Screaming, Can You Hear Me?

I AM SCREAMING LORD, I NEED HELP! My situation is too big for me.

In the Spirit, each of us also play the game of life and the opponent is our flesh, the world (life, situations, circumstances, even tragedy), the devil, and his demons. The acceptance of Christ gives us needed to protect our destiny. When we accept Christ, He is our personal Savior. The Holy Ghost is our reminder and guide, and angels are assigned to guard us, protect us, and rage in battle for us.

John 16:13 says: *Howbeit when he, the Spirit of truth, is come, he will guide you into all truth: for he shall not speak of himself; but whatsoever he shall hear, that shall he speak: and he will shew you things to come.*

Without Christ, we have no protection and the enemy can ultimately damage or destroy our queen *destiny*.

I AM SCREAMING LORD; I need your help!!! I would that we realize the enemy in our life can be anyone or anything causing us not to reach our goals and purpose. We give the devil more credit than he deserves. According to the Word of God, *we have power over the enemy. Jesus rose with all power in His hand.* Whatever we bless will be blessed, and whatever we curse will be cursed, if we are living according to the promises in the Word of God.

PRESENT STATE
Chapter Two

This chapter focuses on life challenges and obstacles and how they cause us to react in our emotions instead of the Word of God. Our "norm" may not be our neighbor's norm and therefore we have to use the Word of God to rightly divide the Word of truth. This mean that we can use the Word of God in our situations in life that will help us get to the place where our screams will turn into prophetic truths based on the Word of God.

MY SPIRIT

I AM SCREAMING BECAUSE of my condition. I do not know how I got this way. I awoke Spiritually and realize that I am not in the place I am supposed to be according to the Word of God.

Psalm 51:1-4 says: *Have mercy on me, O God, according to your unfailing love; according to your greatest compassion blot out my transgressions. Wash away all my iniquity and cleanse me from my sin. For I know my transgressions, and my sin is always before me. Against you, you only, have I sinned and done what is evil in your sight: that thou mightiest be justified when thou speaketh, and be clear* *when thou judgest.*

Life has pressed us many times because of our many experiences. We wound up in a strange land and are not sure where to set up our camp.

I AM SCREAMING, CAN YOU HEAR ME? Our condition finds us in a place with little joy, little peace, and a tad bit of praise, but if we have to deal with one more thing we are not going to make it.

LORD, I AM SCREAMING because of my condition. I do not know how to pick myself up from this valley I find myself in. Have you ever tried taking your position in life as the Word of God says? Situations sometimes calls for us to step back and let God take control, but because it is so uncomfortable, we continue to do what is familiar.

LORD, I AM SCREAMING, CAN YOU HEAR ME? After so much time spent doing it my own way, I have convinced myself that my way is still the way, although clearly, it is not working.

Have you considered that going through the same situation for so long; that perhaps you do not deserve good things? We are buried in a world of sin and have stopped fighting because the god of this world has blinded our eyes to what od has said about our life and situation.

The Word, our confession, the blood of Jesus, and being our brother's keeper are our tools that ensures our victory, but if we choose not to utilize our tools; the enemy creeps in and destroy us using whatever tactics he can. Salvation is a gift and we must know that it is not something we work for. We must accept the gift from Jesus, and we must realize God loves us unconditionally.

The *norm* looks differently for each of us. My scream and your scream will be heard but sound differently. For instance, we all know that a person who has seemingly nothing going for himself, while the next person, is doing something positive and his life is headed somewhere up. The two connect and finds an opening in each other's life and pretends to be friends.

I AM SCREAMING, CAN YOU HELP ME?
That is why the Word of God tells us to know those that dwell among us. We cannot operate outside the Word of God and think we will win because that means we are not covered by the blood of Jesus. Operating in the Word does not allow the enemy to attack us in the way the enemy wants. Remember the purpose of the enemy is to steal, kill, and destroy.

BLINDED MIND
Perhaps we've all heard that perception is reality.

How we look at things are as important as it impacts our decision making process. The power of perception is directly tied to our mindset because how we look at a situation will determine what steps we take next. There is a famous saying; "Believe none of what you hear and half of what you see. Is it possible for the mind to deceive us? The correct answer is yes. When we rehearse a scenario again and again, we can see that situation just the way we perceived it in our minds. That is why the Word of God tells us to renew our mind daily. In addition, the word tells us that the heart is deceitfully wicked. However, the word does give us a solution, which is giving our heart to Jesus. He will make everything alright.

Perception is reality, and the way we see things for us is the way it is. So how many of us can say that the way we see things is always the way it is? We can all conclude that the answer is no because the mind is a powerful thing and can be used by the enemy to distract and defeat us when we don't stand on the Word of God.

The mind is the thing that can make or break us. Sometimes we rehearse things over and over until that thing shifts our thought process, thus the enemy preys on that weakness of the mind, knowing we're not strong enough to comprehend it from God's perspective. Being emotional creatures, we second guess the very sure things of God, which keeps us focused on the crisis rather than the Christ! In this *state*, we don't see past how we feel without divine counsel. So we definitely need to be in position to receive the help for our situations.

I AM SCREAMING, CAN YOU HEAR ME?

Men and women of God should tell us what we feel we need to hear to make our situation better. However, when the man or woman of God is counseling, he or she is using the Word of God as the standard and speaking from their Spirit to your Spirit. Does anybody understand? Who are we talking to? Again, we are not hearing, and in most cases, we reject the voice of the Spirit.

We are screaming because we do not have much of a personal relationship with Jesus and our lives are turned upside down; go a different course. How do I know this, you ask? Well, the only way we get results is to remove our emotions out of the way and dive into the Holy pages, practicing what we learn. Through the Word, we scope through the lens of the Holy Writ. At the same time, we fellowship in our local assembly and with God, having that pastor who steadily watch for our souls. therefore, that pastor delivers a rhema word to the congregant to digest, and apply. Then watch God workout your problem for your good.

We fall sometimes fall into a rut because of the

things we have seen and experienced; which shapes our beliefs. Our human Spirit's witness says "If we believe it, then we will act on it." Consequently, if we don't believe, we won't act God's Word.

We confess the Word of God over our situation but our *private pauses* is an indication that we really don't believe God is who He say He is. We have to become stewards over the Word of God we confess. To accomplish good stewardship, start by hiding the Word of God in your hearts that you might not sin against God. When situations arise, we will have the anchor need to keep us grounded of what the Word of God says and stand on it, PERIOD. Below are additional Scriptures for reading:

ADDITIONAL SCRIPTURES

St. Matthew 6:34
St. Matthew 13:14
St. Matthew 15:14
I John 2:11
II Peter 1:5-9
Deuteronomy 29:4
Ephesians 4:18
Acts 28:27
I John 2:11
II Corinthians 4:1-6
Isaiah 42:16
Isaiah 59:10

St. Matthew 13:14-15 which states, and the prophecy of Isaiah is fulfilled, which says *"Hearing you will hear and shall not understand, and seeing you will see and not perceive, for the hearts of this people have grown dull. Their ears are hard of hearing, and their eyes they have closed, lest they should see with their eyes and hear with their ears, lest they should understand with their hearts and turn, so that I should heal them."*

For what man knoweth the things of a man, save the Spirit of man which is in him? Even so the things of God knoweth no man, but the Spirit of God
I Corinthians 2:11.

How many times have you seen people operate in ministry and steadily talking about things being done? This person is letting us know that he's not linked in and does not have the same spirit as the leader. There is only one visionary of any congregation and that is the bishop/pastor God has placed in authority.

I AM SCREAMING, BECAUSE I am not a bad person, but I am have gone through some very bad stuff.

James 1: 2-6 says *Consider it pure joy, my brothers, whenever you face trials of many kinds, because you know that the testing of your faith develops perseverance. Perseverance must finish its work so that you may be mature and complete, not lacking anything. If any of you lack wisdom, he should ask God, who gives generously to all without finding fault, and it* *will be given to him. But when he asks, he must believe and not doubt because he who doubts is like a wave of the sea, blown and tossed by the wind.*

Psalm 51:10-12 which says *Create in me a pure heart, O God and renew a steadfast Spirit within me. Do not cast me from your presence or take your Holy Spirit from me. Restore to me the joy of your salvation and grant to me a willing Spirit, to sustain me.*

Even though wrong is done to us, we still have to stand on the integrity of God's word. Emotions shouldn't drive you in a negative place. You do not have the right to retaliate toward that person. You are still held accountable to God. *Owe no man nothing but to love him.* We should re-adjust our thinking that people owe us something if we have not wronged anyone. We feel like if we have not done anything bad then nothing bad should happen to us. However, that is not the way the enemy sees it and despite that belief, that is not the way it is. Not knowing our position is just as damaging as knowing our position and not covering our position. For example, if we are part of a baseball team that is positioned in the outfield, each player has a strategic position so the ball can't pass them. The players are positioned so that with minimum effort they can reach the ball, make the throw, and get the most efficient play. If each player decides not to cover their position, then their position will be compromised, and the ball is hit into the outfield, it goes to the player who is not in position. Every player now has to move out of their position to cover the player's position who is not doing his part. Where there would have been no stress, now stress is present because one player moved out of his position.

In the Spiritual realm, the Lord wants us to be strategically positioned so we can put the devil to flight each time. If we are unaware of things in the Spirit world, how will we be able to fight in the Spirit? Below are additional Scriptures for reading.

ADDITIONAL SCRIPTURES
John 10:10-11
Roman 8:6-7
I Corinthian 3:3
II Corinthians 10:4
Proverbs 23:7

We all have parents or guardian that have taken care of us since birth, grew up in what is called a *normal families*. However, we have to be careful of the definition of normal. What we think is normal may not be normal or very different for another. For example, if a child grows up seeing his parents fighting, though chaotic, it is a normal occurrence because he witnessed regularly. His soul may cry out in frustration knowing that this isn't right, but becomes numb by seeing it many times. Parents are responsible for their children's welfare and help them shape positive value and behaviors. Their mindset can help them or hinder them from their destiny. For others, it seems as though life did not deal them a good hand when it came to parents. Then, there is the other percentage that was just not affected by their situations at all. How could that be? This could be because there are some people that are destined to do certain things in the Kingdom and are preserved and not tarnished by the issues of life. It appears they had some kind of shield of protection and an innate ability to adapt and deal with their life situations. Things we witness and experience tend to become a part of us.

We grow up seeing and believing in things we were taught from birth. As children, we believe our parents/guardians are good, and have our best interest in mind. In the formative years of elementary middle and even high school, it seemed a large majority had the same definitions for things we should and should not do. There were a marginal community that fell through the cracks not being taught a clear sense of morality because of their lack of family values and structure. We define our lives based on our belief and faith.

I AM SCREAMING, CAN YOU HEAR ME? Changingminds.org defines belief as an assumed truth. It further states that we create beliefs to anchor our understanding of the world around us. So once we have formed a belief, we will tend to persevere with that belief. The Merriam-Webster dictionary defines belief as a feeling of being sure that someone or something exists or that something is true: A feeling that something is good, right, or valuable. BibleGateway.com defines faith as being sure of the things we hope for and knowing that something is real even if we do not see it.

Are you in the same place this time as you were last year, the year before and the year before that? Did you know that most of us do not know that *we* set our own standard without sometimes saying a word, because of what we believe? Every action we take has an impact on our life. The most important thing that causes action or reaction is our *mindset*.

If what we believe is true, we will act on it and the opposite is equally plausible: unbelief gets the same result; no action or reaction. This is why the Word of God tells us to *renew our minds daily* in **Ephesians 4:23, Romans 12:2**. However, renewal does not always cause a person to act or react on what is discovered. Sometimes we come to realizations, but feel there is nothing that can be done about what is going on. That is exactly what the enemy wants us to think. As we begin to spend time in the Word of God, our relationship develops, we will learn that we CAN change our situation by speaking the written

Word of God to it.

When we ask Christ to come into our hearts; the Holy Spirit is the One who guides us into all truths. The Holy Spirit is also the One that brings revelation through the Word as we study to show ourselves approved unto God. One revelation that changed my life was when the Holy Spirit expounded the difference between belief and faith. The Holy Spirit re-iterated that we all have the power to believe because it is the written Word of God; but how do we turn belief into faith? You've probably heard the saying 'seeing is believing.' You ask, what does that mean? The Holy Spirit broke this down to me. I almost had an out of body experience. Belief is tangible - knowing something because it is written or you can see or touch it. Faith is lining up our mind and belief with the written Word of God and acting upon it. In other words, knowing the Word is not enough, you must apply the Word in every situation in times when you need it. This is when your belief has developed into faith.

I AM SCREAMING, CAN YOU HEAR ME?
Awesome huh!

It does not matter what is going on in our lives, we never have the right to act outside of the Word of God. Sometimes, we feel that we are justified in retaliation if we are provoked, but if we would remember the Word of God when people do us wrong, we would let God and time handle the situation. Vengeance is the Lord's! However, so many times we revert back to our *old man* (meaning we are doing it the ways we used to before we accepted Christ) especially when we feel like the Lord is not moving fast enough. We are all guilty of this at some point in our walk with Christ. The goal is to grow Spiritually daily. When we repent, we are truly Godly sorry. This means when we find ourselves in the same situation, we should not act the same because Godly repentance brings about a change in our hearts. Our relationship with God is evolving, which helps us to be more accountable to the Word of God.

This comes because we are actively seeking truth, spending time in prayer and the Word of God. We become sensitive and conscious to the things of the Spirit. A personal relationship with Jesus will allow the Holy Spirit to reign in our lives even when the *old man* tries to rise up.

Do you remember when you first met that person you knew you wanted to get to know and be with for the rest of your life? You invested time talking, learning, and gathering. While getting to know one another, you were not privy to things that were offensive to each of you, but as time progressed, spending considerable amounts of time together, you quickly learned things that were offensive to each of you. As our relationship progresses in God, we are held accountable because we choose to walk in the Word of God.

So this leads us to ask: do you have a belief or faith? Once you identify the answer to the faith / belief question, then you'll be able to tell why you are fighting, knowing, dancing and hoping.

So what does our mindset have to do with our destiny? The mindset determines whether we achieve in the natural or in the Spirit. The Scripture also tells us that *we perish because of a lack of knowledge* **(Hosea 4:6)**. How does information affect our decisions in life? One way, for example, if you want to be a doctor, you researched and discovered you are not good in anatomy. You could be a part of the population that change your major simply because you aren't willing to put an extra effort learning anatomy to accommodate your level of comfort.

Some do not mind doing the things needed to become successful in this world, but when it comes to Spiritual things, it seems we literally want them to drop out of the sky. Additionally, we feel we do not have to make any preparations to operate in the Spirit, but this is far from the truth. We think we are ready in the Spirit to deal with spiritual things. Not knowing how to operate in the Spirit does not exempt us from the devil's attacks. The Word of God says ...*those who hunger and thirst after righteousness shall be filled.* This is a guarantee from the Almighty God. This is the best assurance that anyone can receive; the question is do we believe what the Father said.

I AM SCREAMING, CAN YOU HELP ME?

WHERE ARE WE?
Chapter Three

I AM SCREAMING BECAUSE I cannot seem to get out of my present situation (rut).

Roman 8:1-14 which states: *There is therefore now no more condemnation to them which are in Christ Jesus, who walk not after the flesh, but after the Spirit. For the law of the Spirit of life in Christ Jesus hath made me free from the law of sin and death. For what the law could not do, in that it was weak through the flesh, God sending His Own Son in the likeness of sinful flesh, and for sin, condemned sin in the flesh. That the righteousness of the law might be fulfilled in us, who walk not after the flesh, but after the Spirit. For they that after the flesh do mind the things of the flesh; but they that are after the Spirit, the things of the Spirit. For to be carnally minded is death, but to be Spiritually minded is life and peace. Because the carnal mind is enmity against God: for it is not subject to the law of God, neither indeed can be. So they that are in the flesh cannot please God. But ye are not in the flesh, but in the Spirit, if so be that the Spirit of God dwell in you. Now if any man have not the Spirit of Christ, he is none of his. And if Christ be in you, the body is dead because of sin; but the Spirit is life because of righteousness. But if the Spirit of him that raised up Jesus from the dead dwell in you, he that raised*

Christ from the dead shall also quicken your mortal bodies by his Spirit that dwelleth in you. Therefore, brethren, we are debtors not to the flesh, to live after the flesh. For if ye live after the flesh, ye shall die, but if ye through the Spirit do mortify the deeds of the body, ye shall live. For as many as are led by the Spirit of God, they are the sons of God.

Endorsing our way for so long but getting the same response much of the time tilts the scales to expect negativity. In totality, we've not allowed the blood of Jesus to wash us, nor allowed the preached word to help renew our mindset. We are stuck due to long hurt, loneliness, disappointment which have taken occupancy in our lives. Some actually believe, bad things just seem to find them.

I AM SCREAMING, CAN YOU HEAR ME?

How can the Spirit of the Lord live in us, if we choose to do things opposite of what the Word of God says? The Word tells us good and evil cannot dwell together nor can light and darkness occupy the same space. So we ask the question again, "How can the Spirit of the Lord dwell in our temples unless we allow Him to clean up our body and mind, soul and Spirit? The Word also says that He will keep us if we want to be kept.

From the day we were born, we see things we want and don't want in our lives. However, most times, our decisions aren't based on anything more than what our flesh wanted.

A parent's role is to instruct our children in the admonition of the Lord, so when they are old, they will not depart from those principles, knowing there will be other influences in our precious children's lives. Parents, make a conscience decision to be connected to the source of life GOD. You will help more than just your seed, but those who are connect to your children. The Word of God helps us find our way to Jesus where mercy and grace abide in our time of fellowship or need (**Hebrews 4:12).**

Many struggle with "What is wrong with me?" We often have an inner struggle.

I AM SCREAMING, CAN YOU HEAR ME?
As we continue to grow and mature, we try to figure out why is there a "VOID" in our lives. We realize something is not quite right, but we cannot put our finger on it.

I AM SCREAMING, CAN YOU HELP ME?
You perhaps decide to accept an invitation to go to church with a friend. From the moment you step inside the church, something tugs at your Spirit, but you aren't sure what it is or how to explain it. As the service progresses, you feel kind of weird and don't know what is going on in your heart. Every human spirit longs to be connected to God for a recreated Spirit, and when we are not connected, we feel

incomplete and out of place. Our soul screams because we are not happy, but we are searching for the missing "thing" in our lives.

I AM SCREAMING, CAN YOU HELP ME?

Once accepting Jesus, we realize it was Jesus' way, influences and character, that was missing from our lives. Your way has not achieved what you've needed, nor what your soul is calling for. Accepting Jesus as Lord and Savior is a matter of the heart, and when it is time to come into the kingdom of God, it's like having a transient experience. At last, we have become a part of God's family. The Word of God says that we have become part of the *peculiar people and a royal priesthood* because we joined Jesus as Lord, Savior and Brother.

For some, it was a tactic for us to come to church, and others who had a bad experience and did not want to deal with church or their folks. Our Father knows what to do, who to send, and how to draw each and every one of us. However, the decision to accept or reject Christ is a decision of the heart, and no one can make that decision for you. Will you try His way today (by following the instructions in the Scriptures), but you have been doing it your way for so long and nothing has changed.

I AM SCREAMING, CAN YOU HELP ME?

Have you heard the story about the son who went to his father and asked for his portion? The rich man's son had a right to ask for his inheritance because of who he was and who he was connected to. He left his father's house and went into a strange land. It is not the Father's will that we remain at the house all of our lives. However, He wants to nourish our body, mind, soul and Spirit so that we can win others to Christ. He is reproducing Himself in us to send us so we can be examples, and win others to the body of Christ.

HOW DID WE GET THERE?

I AM SCREAMING BECAUSE I won't obey God's messenger i.e. God's word (Lover of themselves). According to Roman 10:14-18 which says, how then shall they call on Him in whom they have not believed? And how shall they believe in Him of whom they have not heard? And how shall they hear without a preacher? And how shall they preach unless they are sent? As it written, how beautiful are the feet of those who preach the gospel of peace? Who bring glad tidings of good things! But they have not all obeyed the gospel. For Isaiah says, Lord who has blessed our report? So then faith comes by hearing, and hearing by the Word of God.

Sometimes we are so focused on what we feel like doing that we do not allow the Holy Spirit to lead or direct us. When we are focused on ourselves, doing the things we want to do, focus on our own goals instead of the kingdom (winning souls to Christ) does not allow room for the Holy Spirit to guide us unto all truths as the Bible tells us.

2 Timothy 3 : *This know also, that in the last days perilous times shall come. For men shall be lovers of their own selves, covetous, boasters, proud, blasphemers, disobedient to parents, unthankful, unholy, without natural affection, trucebreakers, false accusers, incontinent, fierce, despisers of those that are good, Traitors, heady, high-minded, lovers of pleasures more than lovers of God; Having a form of godliness, but denying the power thereof: from such turn away. For of this sort are they which creep into houses, and lead captive silly women laden with sins, led away with divers lusts, ever learning, and never able to come to the knowledge of the truth. Now as Jannes and Jambres withstood Moses, so do these also resist the truth: men of corrupt minds, reprobate concerning the faith. But they shall proceed no further: for their folly shall be manifest unto all men, as theirs also was. But thou hast fully known my doctrine, manner of life, purpose, faith, longsuffering, charity, patience, Persecutions, afflictions, which came unto me at Antioch, at Iconium, at Lystra; what persecutions I endured: but out of them all the Lord delivered me. Yea, and all that will live godly in Christ Jesus shall suffer persecution. But evil men and seducers shall wax worse and worse, deceiving, and being deceived. But continue thou in the things which thou hast learned and hast been assured of, knowing of whom thou hast learned them; And that from a child thou hast known the Holy*

Scriptures, which are able to make thee wise unto salvation through faith which is in Christ Jesus. All Scripture is given by inspiration of God, and is profitable for doctrine, for reproof, for correction, for instruction in righteousness: That the man of God may be perfect, thoroughly furnished unto all good works.

We have to be open to the Holy Spirit, so that we can hear what the Spirit is saying. Sometimes we think that the pastors/leaders are supposed to do it by themselves. This tells me that we are not following the instructions from the Word of God and do not know what the Word of God says in our specific situations. We are all given our gift for the edifying of the body to the glory of God and to advance the kingdom of God.

Another Scripture that speaks to our situation is

Roman 8: 1-14 *Therefore, there is now no condemnation for those who are in Christ Jesus, because through Christ Jesus the law of the Spirit who gives life has set you free from the law of sin and death. For what the law was powerless to do because it was weakened by the flesh, God did by sending his own Son in the likeness of sinful flesh to be a sin offering. And so he condemned sin in the flesh. In order that the righteous requirement of the law might be fully met in us, who do not live according to the flesh but according to the Spirit. Those who live according to the flesh have their minds set on what the flesh desires; but those who live in accordance with the Spirit have their minds set on what the Spirit desires. The mind governed by the flesh is death, but the mind governed by the Spirit is life* *and peace. The mind governed by the flesh is hostile to God; it does not submit to God's law, nor can it do so. Those who are in the realm of the flesh cannot please God. You, however, are not in the realm of the flesh but are in the realm of the Spirit, if indeed the Spirit of God lives in you. And if anyone does not have the Spirit of Christ, they do not belong to Christ. But if Christ is in you, then even though your body is subject to death because of sin, the Spirit gives life because of righteousness. And if the Spirit of him who raised Jesus from the dead is living in you, he who raised Christ from the dead will also give life to your mortal bodies because of the Spirit who lives in you. Therefore, brothers and sisters, we have an obligation—but it is not to the flesh, to live according to it. For if you live according to the flesh, you will die; but if by the Spirit you put to death the misdeeds of the body, you will live. For those who are led by the Spirit of God are the children of God.*

In some instances, when we have been doing "a thing" for such a long time, we feel that we cannot recover. We also feel that we deserve what we get because of what we have been doing. Let us thank God that our Savior, Jesus does not feel that way about us. There is nothing we can do to deserve salvation; salvation is a GIFT from God. We cannot work to get it; it is a gift from the Father above. However, we have to look at it for what it is; a gift. The Bible says that He places before us death and life, He would that we would choose life. The Word of God says that if we have to accept Jesus in our hearts and believe that God raise Jesus from the dead, We

SHALL be saved.

Romans 10:9 says: *That if thou shalt confess with thy mouth the Lord Jesus, and shalt believe in thine heart that God hath raised him from the dead, thou shalt be saved.*

I believe that as we develop our relationship with Jesus, the Holy Spirit will bring all things to our remembrance so that we can win in every situation in our lives. We have to know the Scripture that helps us realize our lives are lost unless we believe and know what the Word of God says about our lives.

THERE IS NO WAY FOR OUR FAITH TO GROW UNLESS WE FIND OURSELVES IN SITUATIONS WHERE WE CAN APPLY THE WORD AND WATCH THE WORD WORK IN AND FOR US.

God never told us that when we go through, it would be comfortable, He just assured us a way of escape. The Word of God tells us that there has no temptation taken you but such as common to man; this tells me the Creator knows the things we will be faced with, however, He will make a way of escape. This is our "assurance policy" from our Father. **1**

Corinthians 10:13 says: *No temptation has overtaken you except what is common to mankind. And God is faithful; he will not let you be tempted beyond what you can bear. But when you are tempted, he will also provide a way out so that you can endure it.*

When God appoints, He anoints! We must not question God! He knows and cares about us. We cannot think that we are able to measure up to those appointed pastors, teachers, preachers, bishops, lay members, intercessors, praise and worship leaders, etc.

The Word of God gives us to know that our gift will make room for us, but there are so many of us who try to covet another brother's or sister's gift.

Realizing in the spirit of our own flesh, our gift lay dormant without ever being developed. Nonetheless, if each of us can get a revelation through the Word of God and use the it to assist us, we will recognize and win in our own battles. In our frailty, we can become comfortable with everyone else's gift because the Word of God has made known to us that our gift will make room for us. So many times we do not have faith in what the Word of God says because we are so easily distracted by people, circumstances, burdens and ultimately the cares of this life. The things that we go through take our joy, our happiness, our dance, our shout and our strength. Yes, we have and know the answer, but our situation cannot change if we don't believe in the WORDS we are speaking.

It takes consistency and determination in the WORD to keep us focused on what God is saying about our lives. If we do not know how to fight our battles using the Word of God; there can arise obstacles which will ultimately cripple us from getting to our destiny.

ADDITIONAL SCRIPTURES:
Psalm 19:7-14
Ephesians 4:29-32
Proverbs 9:10

Because of circumstances in our lives, we decide by *actions* to give up. How do you know when someone has given up? One way to tell is the constant repeat of patterns again and again. The reasoning behind this behavior is familiarity.

I AM SCREAMING, CAN YOU HELP ME?
They've tried it their parent's way; this way; and that way; and their friend's way. Nothing is changing so they stick with a pattern that is familiar and comfortable with even though it doesn't work.

The only way we will know if we have failed is by the standards we set for ourselves, and we will know we have failed when we apply the standard of God's Word. God knows all things. We have to accept

Christ our Lord and Savior and the final authority. Essentially, allowing God to direct our steps means we can win EVERY battles and situations.

We lose control (temper, words, actions, etc.) sometimes which causes us to our families, jobs, our own life, etc.

We get to that place because of what we've come to believe. The enemy does not want us to understand the magnitude of God's love for us, so he continually place things before our eyes based on our thinking and actions. In James from the Scriptures, we are told that *if we lack wisdom in anything, then just ask God for wisdom* on how to deal with situations and people.

Let's face it, our parents had their own way of doing things, and since that was what we saw much of our lives; has transferred now to how we deal with things. Let me ask you, are your parents' way of doing things based on the Word of God? I will let you be the judge of that.

In addition, another way you can judge is by your own circumstances. We sometimes feel if someone has done us wrong, then we are justified to do them wrong back, but the Word of God tells us that vengeance is the Lord's and He will repay. Sometimes it is good to just keep silent because even as Christians, we sometimes do not express things we say in the right spirit; and this causes contentions between or among our family and friends, brothers and sisters in Christ.

I AM SCREAMING, CAN YOU HELP ME? HOW CAN WE GET BACK?

We often feel because we have strayed so far away from what our parents have taught us, we internalize no one will love us and the ones that used to don't anymore. However, take a moment and reflect on the story of the prodigal son who came to his senses and realized he needed to go back to his father and repent. The prodigal son said he would rather be a hired hand for his father than stay in his present "state" in order to obtain the basic essentials in life. When the father saw his son coming home from afar, he started celebrating. The one who was lost is found. We sometimes know the things we are doing are wrong, but the sin that dwells in us causes us to continue on the destructive path.

I AM SCREAMING, CAN YOU HELP ME?

The father was glad that his son had come home and took his place as the eldest son. The enemy's purpose is to keep us from realizing the surmountable degree of love God has for us. The One who gave His only begotten Son to die for the world! If we would remember the Prodigal Son, and know that God's love is unconditional; we would be able to allow the anointing of God to reign supreme in our lives, even when we do not understand what is going on.

We can get back to the place we have been

searching for by allowing the Lord to be God in our lives. Let me explain. God is always waiting with his arms wide open waiting for us to repent. However, the enemy tries to keep us from the Father's arms, love and word by keeping us focusing on life situations. The enemy does not want us to realize our full potential, purpose or realize the magnitude of God's love for us. The Word of God constantly tells what the cure for each situation that we face. As we continually develop our relationship with Jesus, our Savior through the Word of God, we will see that we can win in life. By winning, we mean that we will be able to recognize the tactics of the enemy because we are in communication with our Savior through the Word of God.

SOCIETY POSITION AND EXPECTATION

So often we allow society to dictate what we do in our lives instead of seeking the awesomeness of God and His Will for our lives. We are spirit-beings living in a carnal world. Depending on pedigree, locality, the color of our skin and ethnicity, society has placed stigmas and prejudices on us, our children, and our future generations. Consequently, we start to live by the rules and standards of the world. But because of Jesus, we are no longer categorized with people in the world. We are now a peculiar people, a royal priesthood; partakers as the children of God.

For example, when we get married, we adopt the

world's mentality (before we accepted Jesus as our Lord and Savior) because research says that half of marriages end in divorce, and because we are not focusing on what the Word of God says about marriage. Marriage is a covenant relationship and there are instructions in the Word of God regarding the man and woman's roles. What we are saying is that if we do not have a foundation, which is the Word of God; then we are more likely to see a higher divorce rate.

I AM SCREAMING, CAN YOU HEAR ME?

This means that we have to search the Word of God so we can develop our personal relationship with Christ. Therefore, we will become more accountable based on the Word of God. The Word of God says that we perish for the lack of knowledge.

DOING MORE WITH LESS

In this society, indirectly, and directly it can be perceived that if we do not have a certain amount of money, or live in a certain neighborhood then we do not have anything going for us. Let the truth be told, if money is everything, then why are so many rich those who have money and can buy or live where they want, commit suicide at higher rates. According to article entitled "Why suicides are more common in richer neighborhoods" reported the people tend to commit suicide because they are comparing themselves to others and believing they are coming up short, and not able to face who they really have become. In addition, the author quoted "A newspaper from the San Francisco Federal Reserve shows that, all else being equal, suicide risks are higher in wealthier neighborhoods, a morbid demonstration of the folly of trying to "*keep up with the Joneses.*" (Sanburn) This should let all of us know that money is not the first thing to get, because the Word declared *above all thy getting, get an understanding.* If we as Christians and Kingdom Builders would decide to live by the Word of God instead of embracing our circumstances, we would draw more people to God, church, then more people would accept Jesus as their personal Savior. Decisions would be more sound if we based our decisions on the Bible instead of emotions. What a rewarding life to have!

I AM SCREAMING, CAN YOU HEAR ME?

Let us be clear: there is nothing wrong with money. However, understand that there is a spirit behind money. Additionally, the Word of God says *the love of money is the root of all evil.* Once we understand that God's intent and interest *are good and not evil* according to **Jeremiah 29:11**; we will always want to honor Him first by tithing. To tithe means to bring 10% of what you earn to the church so the visionary can carry out the things the Lord has led him to. We have to honor the commandment of the Lord and allow the church to be accountable to God how they spend the money they receive.

Malachi 3: 8-12: *Will a man rob God? Yet ye have robbed me. But ye say, Wherein have we robbed thee? In tithes and offerings. Ye are cursed with a curse: for ye have robbed me, even this whole nation. Bring ye all the tithes into the storehouse, that there may be meat in mine house, and prove me now herewith, saith the Lord of hosts, if I will not open you the windows of Heaven, and pour you out a blessing, that there shall not be room enough to receive it. And I will rebuke the devourer for your sakes, and he shall not destroy the fruits of your ground; neither shall your vine cast her fruit before the time in the field, saith the Lord of hosts. And all nations shall call you blessed: for ye shall be a delightsome land, saith the Lord of hosts.*

It is our job to give our tithes and we try to do what God has called others to do and forget what we are supposed to do such as give and love. When we are not focused on our purpose as the Word of God is planted in our Spirits; the enemy come in and steal what has been planted.

LORD I AM SCREAMING, CAN YOU HEAR AND HELP ME?

One thing we have realized is we must align our lives with the instructions in the Word of God. The Father wants to shower blessings on us, He speaks through His Word; He also sees us through the blood of Jesus. He gave His only Son for each of us.

TITHING? YEA OR NAY

TITHING IS NOT AN OPTION; IT IS A COMMAND. Some say because this Scripture is located in Malachi, then it must be under the Old Testament laws. However, in II Corinthians it again talks about tithing. Let us not get stuck being ritualistic (doing thing a certain way). Pursue your purpose for which God created.

LORD I AM SCREAMING, CAN YOU HEAR ME?

Tithing unto God is a part of our spiritual worship and reasonable service. We cannot come into the presence of God unless we repent of all our sins knowingly and unknowingly. Repent means that we have searched the Word of God and realize we are doing things opposite of how the Word of God tells. According to gotquestions.org: in the Bible, the word repent means *to change one's mind.* The Bible also tells us that true repentance will result in a change of actions (**Luke 3:8-14; Acts 3:19**). **Acts 26:20** declares, *I preached that they should repent and turn to God and prove their repentance by their deeds.*

The full Biblical definition of repentance is a change of mind that results in a change of action. We ask the Father for forgiveness and change our actions to meet the expectations set forth in the Word of God.

Go to your pastor and find out what is the stance on tithing. I do not believe that he will tell you it is wrong because it is not. There are things that we are expecting and believing God for, and as those things come forth, we have to make sure we align our minds and actions with God's instructions are.

Some have tithed, prayed, given, sown and the things desired, have not yet manifested. There is one thing that is not being taught that will ensure you get what the Word of God declares you can have, and that is fasting. According to United Church of God: For Spiritual purposes, it means to go without eating and drinking (Esther 4:16). Fasting has been a subject that has been neglected for such a long time, but it is the quickest way to get the answer to the questions we have. In the natural, we can arrange things the way we want people to see them, but we cannot change the way things are in our mind or Spirit. Whatever our mindset is, our actions will show. What is your mindset?

I AM SCREAMING BECAUSE I give my tithes and offerings, but my prayers are not answered.

I John 3:19-22 says: *For if our heart condemn us, God is greater than our heart, and knoweth all things. Beloved, if our heart condemn us not, then have we confidence toward God. And whatsoever we ask, we receive of him, because we keep his commandments, and do those things that are pleasing in his* *sight.*

We want the blessing without following the instructions to receive the blessings according to the Word. We have to be willing to check our spirit and ensure we are in line with the Word. The Scripture says: *And hereby we know that we are of the truth, and shall assure our hearts before him.* In addition, **Psalm 27:4** says: *One thing have I desired of the Lord, that will I seek after; that I may dwell in the house of the Lord all the days of my life, to behold the beauty of the Lord, and to enquire in his temple.* If this is your desire, the Scripture gives us detailed instructions from the foundation of the world. Keep in mind our flesh is not in line with the Word of God.

1 Corinthians 2:11 says: *For what man knoweth the things of a man, save the Spirit of man which is in him? Even so the things of God knoweth no man, but the Spirit of God.*

Romans 8:14 *For as many as are led by the Spirit of God, they are the sons of God.*

Proverbs 20:27 *The Spirit of man is the candle of the Lord, searching all the inward parts of the belly.*

Know that the Scriptures, prayer and some discipline in fasting is the answer to our needs; whether we believe or not, He cannot lie.

I AM SCREAMING BECAUSE my perception is not

what the Word says, but I can see "this" or "that" thing in my mind the way I want.

John 12:40, *He hath blinded their eyes, and hardened their heart; that they should not see with their eyes, nor understand with their heart, and be converted, and I should heal them.*

We have been developing our opinion about what life should be since the day we were born. As we grow and observe all the people in our lives, we pick up the things deemed important. Conversely, are these things according to our earthly parents, or on the Word of God. At this present time, we allow society to dictate much of how and who we are, even in the Christian world. Why do you say this?

The divorce rate is just as high if not higher in Christendom than in the secular world. Christians are getting away from the instructions of God regarding the marriage covenant. The church has lost its power because it has taken focus off Jesus and placed emphasis on ourselves.

We could probably agree that sometimes the blows in life catch us off guard, and our response may not always be the right or appropriate one in certain situations. However, when we respond wrong, we can go to our Father that will provide help in the time of trouble. The same Scripture tells us that Jesus was in all points touched with whatever we are going through (Hebrews 4:15-16). This indicates that there is nothing that we can go to God that Jesus cannot speak on our behalf except blasphemy. In addition, once we learn how to be "naked and unashamed" meaning that we can go to the throne without covering any part of us up and because we are honest and we are not lukewarm, God can use us. He said that if we are lukewarm, He will spew us out of His mouth. However, if we are either hot or cold, He can work with us in that state because of our honesty.

Some things apply to us because of our heritage in Jesus, then other things apply because people work the "principle" because you know through personal conviction that a particular principle works. There are people who are not members of any church but their parents have passed down the principle of tithing and those people have witnessed their parents become and remained successful and prosperous because they apply the principle of tithing. However there are people that are not members of any local assembly nor do they believe that they have to be. However, most of us were taught to attend church regularly and tithe unto the Lord because the Word of God commands us to which given to us in the book of Malachi Chapter 3. So, in addition to the principles of tithing, we receive the things God has for us because we are taught and then apply the Word of God to every situation. We believe the words that the Bible declares. The Scripture tells us that if we can conceive it, then God can do above what we are able to perceive.

Ephesians 3: 17-20: *That Christ may dwell in your hearts by faith; that ye, being rooted and grounded in love, May be* *able to comprehend with all saints what is the breadth, and length, and depth, and height; And to know the love of Christ, which passeth knowledge, that ye might be filled with all the fullness of God. Now unto him that is able to do exceeding abundantly above all that we ask or think, according to the power that worketh in us.*

There is no lack in God except when we do not follow and/or believe the commands in the Word of God.

THE CHRONICLE OF OUR CRIES
Chapter Four

MIND

I AM SCREAMING BECAUSE I don't know how to move.

Psalms 111:10 states, *the fear of the Lord is the beginning of wisdom: a good understanding have all they that do his commandments: His praise endureth forever.*

When fear grips our soul, we will not believe the Word of God. In addition, fear will never allow us to reach our potential; without a personal Savior; Jesus the Lord of everything we do. We may believe we can do everything ourselves, but the fact of the matter is there is no one person that made it where they are by themselves. The Lord allows people to see us through the anointing God's Word.

Have you ever heard old people (grandma and granddad) say that child you have a special call or anointing on your life. However, there are some of us who never got a chance to hear that from our grandparents, but we have been experiencing an emptiness that only Jesus can fill. There are times that even those of us who are and have been saved or a while experience emptiness inside. That is the tugging for us to seek God even more and be a living epistle of what the Word of God says. More importantly, that is a call from our Spiritual man for more fellowship with our Heavenly Father, so He can unveil some things in and through our lives. Some of us give God one purpose and that is regulate our Spirits when it comes to Spiritual things, but God is trying to get us to understand that He is concerned about our whole man; our body, mind, soul and Spirit.

Proverbs 14:27 states, *the fear of the Lord is a fountain of life, to depart from the snares of death.*

When we get the revelation of how much God really loves us, the realization can be overwhelming with emotions because we realize that He (Jesus) did not have to die for us. The Word of God tells us that God loves us so much that He gave His only begotten son, that whosoever believe in Him should have everlasting life. Personally, the closest I came to put it in term that I truly understand is when I was watching my daughter interact with her dad. She displayed a different kind of love towards her dad than she did towards me. I really did not understand why she does not love me like that. The Holy Spirit said to me, you see how much your daughter loves her dad, magnify that to infinity and then you will begin to understand how much God loves you.

In our society, much education should equate to a lot of money because we are all seeking ways that we can impact our lives by obtaining money which would change our financial positions, or so we think. If that is what you believe, then let me ask YOU a question. Why are there so many people with money that commit suicide? This indicates that money has its place, but also our Savior has His place and there is nothing and no one who can fill that void besides Jesus. As we begin to embark on and on in life, we try to place people, money, drug, sex, etc. in that void just to discover that what we have placed over that void is not working. You cover the wound (situation) after it is dress to heal, but if the wound (situation) is just covered and never treated, it (the situation) can become in a worst state versus seeking help for whatever is wrong naturally or Spiritually. In the Spirit, it is the same, our Spirit has to be fed in order to grow. If your Spirit is being fed with Word of God by ministers, they your relationships can heal.

> **Galatians 5:16** *This I say then, walk in the Spirit and ye shall not fulfill the lust of the flesh.*

We often quote the Scripture that we are Spiritual being, but do we live like we are Spiritual beings. It takes time and diligence to get to the place where we allow God to really rule our Spirits. We all spend so much time indulging in this world because we have needs to operate here; however, where we are should not overshadow who we are in the Spirit. But, oftentimes it does and we have to get our Spirit to a place where we see that. We usually wake up when we find ourselves in a situation that we cannot get ourselves out of. It is during this time that we seek for our Savior because we now know that we cannot see life without someone, something to rescue us from our present state. We all can agree because we really did not realize how much we need God until the very thing we feared the most comes upon us such as death, divorce, lack, job issues, etc. It just seems like that open up doors to other things happening in our lives. Our parents taught us what they knew, and we value those things. However, we need something more to get us through the rough times in our lives. We all have had a "trying time in our lives and was not in the best state to die; however, we knew Jesus as our Lord and Savior but not as ruler of our life which caused us to feel helpless. We felt that He could/would control our Spirit and we would control the rest. It was not until we began to develop our personal relationship with Jesus that we realize that He is concerned about every part of us. We have to decide to yield our lives to Him (Jesus). Once we begin to develop our personal relationship with Jesus, we will realize how much He loves and cares for us. YES, He is concerned about each and every one of us.

Psalms 51 states our condition in a way no other

Scripture does when it tells us that *we are born into a world of sin,* and there is nothing we can do about our condition but place ourselves in the bosom of the almighty God. In Psalm 51, David asks God to have mercy on him. When we learn how to be naked and unashamed, meaning we do not try to cover what is wrong in our lives, we will begin to move forth in God. We spend so much time trying to cover everything instead of seeking help in the time of need.

Hebrews 4:16 *Let us then approach God's throne of grace with confidence, so that we may receive mercy and find grace to help us in our time of need.*

Sometimes fear will grip us and cause us not to focus on what the Word of God. Our belief comes into action because we can find the in the Word of God whatever the ailment of our condition, but sometimes more work is required for us to move from the valley of despair. Consequently, because we do not fight, we become stuck because of how our circumstances and situation have impacted our minds and Spirits. Instead we focus on our situations more than we focus on the Word of God which gives us our Spiritual medicine,

The Word of God declares that we exist, move and having our being because we allow the Lord to operation unconditionally in our bodies, mind, soul and Spirit. This means that because we are no long in the "driver's" seat of our lives, we sometimes will not understand the move of God in our lives. However, we can be assured that it is the Father at work in our lives. Because we have said "Yes" for the final time, we can confidently, walk in our calling and assignment in the natural and Spirit. God knows the most intimate detail that even our significant other does not know nor understand. We all sometimes get caught up in what we are going through, but it does not, nor can it keep us down. Let Him reign today; He wants to bless you! Prosper you! Give you all that He has prepared from the foundation of the world.

ADDITIONAL SCRIPTURES
Proverbs 3:5-6
St. Luke 12:29
Roman 12:2
II Timothy 1:7
Isaiah 26:3
Roman 8:27
Colossians 3:2
Psalms 17:4-8
Jeremiah 10:23

MIND/SPIRIT
I AM SCREAMING BECAUSE I need a new mind set (renew mind daily).

Romans 12:1-2 says *"I beseech you brethren, by the mercies of God, that you present your bodies, a living sacrifice, holy, acceptable to God, which is your reasonable service. And* *do not be conformed to this world, but be ye transformed by the renewing of your mind, that you may prove what is that good and acceptable and perfect will of God.*

Our mindset will make us or break us, and we have to get to the place where our belief of the written Word of God turn into faith operating in our circumstances and situations in our lives. From the time we are born, we begin to adopt and adapt based on our environment. We develop and a change based on what our mind tells us is correct or incorrect. We allow people in and trust people so much that in addition to our own mindset, people tell us what they think and we take their word as law in our lives. Not realize that all of us have our own opinion and that we all respond differently in each situation. Until we allow God to be God even in our uncomfortable ness, then we will experience defeat in many parts of our lives. Sometimes we need space to experience a little discomfort so that we can get ourselves together.

ADDITIONAL SCRIPTURES:
II Timothy 1:6-7
Psalms 119:93
Isaiah 43:18-19

MIND
I AM SCREAMING BECAUSE I keep going through the same thing over and over and over again.

II Corinthians 10:4-6 says: *For the weapons of our warfare are not carnal but mighty in God for pulling down strongholds. Casting down arguments and every high thing that exalts itself against the knowledge of God, bringing every thought into captivity to the obedience of Christ. And being ready to punish all obedience when your obedience is fulfilled.*

The Word of God declares that there is no temptation that has taken man such as common to man, but He did assure us that He would make a way of escape. Sometimes, we forget that the battle is a Spiritual and not physical, but whether we remember or not the Spiritual fight is still always going on. When we are not aware that there is a fight going on our lives start to become unraveled. Then our Spiritual senses start to kick in and then we say; what is going on? Just because we decide not to join the fight, does not mean that the fight ceases. When people become our focus, then we see to make people happy. But when God become our focus and we surrender ALL to God, then He becomes our focus which mean when things do not go right we seek what God said about that particular situation from the Word of God. Remember that from the time we are born, we are picking up habits from everything, and everybody that we come in contact with. In most cases, we have not accepted Jesus as our Lord and Savior. We go to head start, kindergarten, first-through twelfth grade on to college and at this point most of us go to church, but a mere fraction of us really have a personal relationship with Jesus. When we do not have a relationship with someone, we tend to do whatever we want with no accountability. However, we begin to get to know people and now a relationship is being developed, we become a little more conscious of the things that we do. As our relationship develops, and grows with that person, we deem them to be important to us and we want to be more conscious because we do not want to hurt that person. Hello, the same thing happens as we accept Jesus, read the Word of God, and go to church to hear the preacher/pastor expound on the Word of God. As we begin to learn more about who Jesus is and what He has done for us, we become more sensitive to the Holy Spirit. The Holy Spirit, is our keeper, so that we will not do those things that we once did because once we accept Jesus we become more are aware of Spiritual things because of our personal relationship with Jesus.

The enemy's purpose is not to allow us to really understand or perceive the love that God really has for us. Once we understand God's love for us, we run to Jesus because His arms are outstretched and we can take confidence in Jesus and live. Things are not always going to go right, but we will begin to understand when things go wrong, and know the "how" they went wrong, and "why" of what has happened. Remember, we all want the life that the Bible speaks about that is in Jesus, but we do not know how to ask for it. We think there is some mystical thing when the Word of God says that Jesus is standing at the door of our hearts knocking, knocking, and knocking, until we let Him in. Can't you feel Him knocking, and if you are already saved, can't you feel Him calling you up higher. He is calling us up high, higher, higher, because HE wants to bless and wants to bless us abundantly, above all that we can ask or perceive. Why, do we treat our Savior with such dishonor? He's calling. Won't you answer?

Let's look at **Titus 3:5-6** which says: *He saved us, not because of righteous things we had done, but because of His mercy.*

He saved us through the washing, rebirth and renewal by the Holy Spirit.

MIND
I AM SCREAMING BECAUSE I let people make more of my decisions and I am the one who is living this life.

1 Corinthians 2:11 says*: For who knows a person's thoughts except their own Spirit within them? In the same way no one knows the thoughts of God except the Spirit of God.*

When it comes to people, we allow them to make decisions for us in so many areas of our lives. We place more value on man's words, and we consider them to be more of a law and standard than we place on the Word of God. One reason that this happens is because we can see man. It is crucial that we hear God before we speak a word in any person's life. We are accountable for the things that we say, God said. We have to come to the conclusion that this walk with God is a faith walk and we have to spend some time in the presence of the Lord to initiate the change that we so desire. It takes work and being obedience to the Word of God; allowing God to move us from the stagnant places in our lives. However, if we allow God to take us through the pruning process; it will not easy, sometimes, we feel like we can take the negative things in our lives because we are accustomed to it especially since it has been for so long. But the Word of God says in Revelation 3:20: Here I am! I stand at the door and knock. If anyone hears my voice and opens the door, I will come in and eat with Him, and He with me. So there the Word of God declares that anyone can ask Jesus to come into their heart and He will come in and eat with that person and that person will eat with Jesus (commune). Does Jesus sound like a person that discriminate based on money, color, ethnicity, etc.? He is the richest person we know, one who anyone can go to and He will help that person. We have to realize that other people are trying to live their lives so they can make it to Heaven.

ADDITIONAL SCRIPTURE:
Romans 1:24-25

MIND

I AM SCREAMING BECAUSE I need a breakthrough because I know I am on my way to hell and I do not know how to turn around. I John 1: 9 says: If we confess our sins, he is faithful and just to forgive us our sins, and to cleanse us from all unrighteousness). All of us were on our way to Hell before we accepted Jesus in our hearts and as Lord of our lives. Come to the realization that God is not a respecter of persons. For the Scripture Acts 10:34: Then Peter began to speak: "I now realize how true it is that God does not show favoritism. This means that everyone has to do the same thing to get to the Father. In John 14:6 says: Jesus answered, "I am the way and the truth and the life. No one comes to the Father except through me.

IT DOES NOT MATTER WHO YOU ARE, IF YOU ARE GOING TO HEAVEN, YOU WILL HAVE TO ACCEPT JESUS INTO YOUR HEART.

Additional Scripture:
Colossians 1:20-23

MIND

I AM SCREAMING BECAUSE the people who try to help I push them away, those who hurt me I pull them closer.

Roman 8:1-14 which states: *There is therefore now no more condemnation to them which are in Christ Jesus, who walk not after the flesh, but after the Spirit. For the law of the Spirit of life in Christ Jesus hath made me free from the law of sin and death. For what the law could not do, in that it was weak through the flesh, God sending His Own Son in the likeness of sinful flesh, and for sin, condemned sin in the flesh. That the righteousness of the law might be fulfilled in us, who walk not after the flesh, but after the Spirit. For they that after the flesh do mind the things of the flesh; but they that are after the Spirit, the things of the Spirit. For to be carnally minded is death, but to be Spiritually minded is life and peace. Because the carnal mind is enmity against God: for it is not subject to the law of God, neither indeed can be. So they that are in the flesh cannot please God. But ye are not in the flesh, but in the Spirit, if so be that the Spirit of God dwell in you. Now if any man have not the Spirit of Christ, he is none of his. And if Christ be in you, the body is dead because of sin; but the Spirit is life because of righteousness. But if the Spirit of him that raised up Jesus from the dead dwell in you, he that raised Christ from the dead shall also quicken your mortal bodies by his Spirit that dwelleth in you. Therefore, brethren, we are debtors not to the flesh, to live after the flesh. For if ye live after the flesh, ye shall die, but if ye through the Spirit do mortify the deeds of the body, ye shall live. For as many as are led by the Spirit of God, they are the sons of God.*

Sometimes we want people to tell us what we want to hear, but a 'true" man or woman of God cannot and will not do that. We all are ambassadors of Christ, and as an ambassador, we have certain requirements and expectations that we have to abide by. As our relationship with God develops; we will begin to commune with the Father to hear what He is saying about any and everything in our lives.

ADDITIONAL SCRIPTURE:
Roman 7

BODY

I AM SCREAMING BECAUSE if I do not change, my children are going to end up like me; broken, busted and disgusted.

Luke 12:47: *And that servant, which knew his lord's will, and prepared not himself, neither did according to his will, shall be beaten with many stripes.*

For most of us *norm* is what we witness growing up every day in our own household.

Joel 1:3 *Tell ye your children of it, and let your children tell their children, and their children another generation.*

Know that when we accept Jesus Christ as our Personal Savior "this gives us the right to passage for change" in our lives. We often think that because we were born in a certain condition or mindset that we cannot change or come up out of our present condition, but I am here to tell you can because Jesus

YET lives, you can rise above your circumstances.

Matthew 19:14: *But Jesus said, Suffer little children, and forbid them not, to come unto me: for of such is the kingdom of Heaven.*

How can we tell what we do not know; the only thing we know is that we have a void and trying to fill the void with any and everything? Then one day, we have an encounter with Jesus and our lives will never be the same again. We can all agree that every parent want to provide their child/children with everything the child need; both the children we have and other children we may come in contact with that do not have the basic necessities in life. In Jesus, everything that we need to live a life that is pleasing to God and truly acceptable to us. We just need to change our mindset through the Word of God and make up our minds that you are going to do it God's way; then your situation will begin to change because of the Word of God. Start by reading one Scripture at a time and apply that Scripture every time you need to see that hand of God change something in your life; find a church where you can fellowship with "like minded" believers.

If you are a student, then start with your performance in your class. You are to treat that adult the same way you would if you were talking to an adult in your family. Students behavior in class, and do your homework every time because you are performing your assignment as unto God. In other words, do things that you are in control of with a glad heart even if you feel like the teacher is not fair. Usually if you feel this way, there is a battle always going on between good and evil; even if we are not aware of the Spiritual world. If you are working on your job, then represent the Jesus that you serve and do your job as unto the Lord. No one should have to stand over you to do your job. The Word of God says that He is the author and finisher of your faith at the helm of our lives. When we know better, that is when He is expects us to do better. Know that response in the natural situation have Spiritual consequences because usually we do not connect the natural and Spiritual worlds. However, as we begin to take our place as sons and daughter of our Father, we then think about how our behavior affects our father.

ADDITIONAL SCRIPTURES
Psalm 139:23
Ephesian 6:4
Psalm 115:14
Colossians 3:20-21
1 John 2:12
Ephesians 6:1

MIND
I AM SCREAMING BECAUSE I am in my own way.

Ephesians 4:20-25 *says: That, however, is not the way of life you learned. When you heard about Christ and were taught in him in accordance with the truth that is in Jesus. You were taught, with regard to your former way of life, to put off your old self, which is being corrupted by its deceitful desires; 23 to be made new in the attitude of your minds; and to put on the new self, created to be like God in true righteousness and holiness. Therefore, each of you must put off falsehood and speak truthfully to your neighbor, for we are all members of one body.*

We accepted Jesus into our heart so that He can use us to perform His work. Thereby we will become the person that God has ordained us to be. We have to allow Christ in our heart so we can know how to win in life because usually we allow everything else to cause us not to reach our destiny because of decisions that we make based on our circumstance. Also, what we allow people to speak into our lives, and what life brings our way. Living in a natural state causes us to focus on our flesh which means that we will not reach the destiny which God has preordained for us through the Word of God. In this state, we tend to believe the things that people say to us instead of what the Word of God says about our lives and our situations.

Proverbs 18:1 says: *An unfriendly person pursues selfish ends and against all sound judgment starts quarrels.*

The enemy is fighting us so we will not realize how much God really loves us. Thus the enemy goals are to take us so far away from God that we will feel God will not forgive us even if we repent.

In **Roman 6: 1-14** says: *What shall we say, then? Shall we go on sinning so that grace may increase? By no means! We are those who have died to sin; how can we live in it any longer? Or don't you know that all of us who were baptized into Christ Jesus were baptized into his death? We were therefore buried with him through baptism into death in order that, just as Christ was raised from the dead through the glory of the Father, we too may live a new life. For if we have been united with him in a death like his, we will certainly also be united with him in a resurrection like his. For we know that our old self was crucified with him so that the body ruled by sin might be done away with, that we should no longer be slaves to sin—because anyone who has died has been set free from sin. Now if we died with Christ, we believe that we will also live with him. For we know that since Christ was raised from the dead, he cannot die again; death no longer has mastery over him. The death he died, he died to sin once for all; but the life he lives, he lives to God. In the same way, count yourselves dead to sin but alive to God in Christ Jesus. Therefore, do not let sin reign in your mortal body so that you obey its evil desires. Do not offer any part of yourself to sin as an instrument of wickedness, but rather offer yourselves to God as those who have been brought from death to life; and offer every part of yourself to him as an instrument of righteousness. For sin shall no longer be your master, because you are not under the law, but* *under grace.*

You're familiar with someone who just refuses to do what is needed to do in order to have food and shelter. This is not that person but the enemy fighting to destroy the Word of God as it is heard by the believer.

2 Thessalonians 3:6-12 says: *In the name of the Lord Jesus Christ, we command you, brothers and sisters, to keep away from every believer who is idle and disruptive and does not live according to the teaching you received from us. For you yourselves know how you ought to follow our example. We were not idle when we were with you, nor did we eat anyone's food without paying for it. On the contrary, we worked night and day, laboring and toiling so that we would not be a burden to any of you. We did this, not because we do not have the right to such help, but in order to offer ourselves as a model for you to imitate. For even when we were with you, we gave you this rule: "The one who is unwilling to work shall not eat." We hear that some among you are idle and disruptive. They are not busy; they are busybodies. Such people we command and urge in the Lord Jesus Christ to settle down and earn the food they eat.*

MIND

I AM SCREAMING BECAUSE I feel like my husband treats me like a slave, not a help meet.

Proverbs 31:10-16 says: *A wife of noble character who can find? She is worth far more than rubies. Her husband has* *full confidence in her and lacks nothing of value. She brings him well, not harm, all the days of her life. She selects wool and flax and works with eager hands. She is like the merchant ships, bringing her food from afar. She gets up while it is still night; she provides food for her family and portions for her female servants. She considers a field and buys it; out of her earnings she plants a vineyard.*

Sometimes it is not our husbands, but our own perception of ourselves; what we see growing up in our parents' house, what we picked up from the television, or even what we discuss with our friends. We have to know who we are and whose we are before we decided to take on a role that we have no training for ourselves. Any answers we want; we will find it in the Word of God. Sometimes we feel like a slave because we feel like that is what our role is to our husbands, and we have not read the Bible, counseling, nor the Word of God to tell us what our role is in our marriage. In our grandparents' time, we were told what our role was and we stepped into it and had nothing to say and did not challenge what they told us because we trusted the God in them that they were leading us the right way. However, times have changed but the Word of God nor God's instructions from the Word of God has not changed to help us in our lives. The Word has sustained generations and generations of people and it we would put the Word of God to the test, it will sustain us. Sometimes we are so focused on what our spouses are not doing, that we never take time to appreciate the things that they are doing. Personally, one of the things that I have learned is that when I find myself complaining so much about my spouse, I am not spending enough time with the Father seeking His wisdom on how to meet the needs of my spouse. We cannot blame someone for the role we take and operate in it without the wisdom needed to fulfill our purpose as the helpmeet of our husbands. We sometimes do not realize that we have become our mothers in a different time and our husbands are a different kind of man of God than our earthly father was. Our parents instill in us what they knew based on what they were taught. We have an advocate which is the Father and the Holy Spirit who will lead us unto ALL truths. Once we become of age, we take what we know and seek out what we do not know so that we can live the life that represents God in every aspect of our lives. Another aspect that impact what we believe is the media. Even as Christians we look at what is called Christian television and base some of our beliefs on what we see on television. The media is no way for anyone to find out what their role is in their marriage. The first thing people tend to say is no; they are not using the television to influence them. However, we have to know that what we watch and listen to are placed in our subconscious mind. We are not saying that you cannot look at television, we are saying that as we watch television and our children, we have to be strategic because there are messages being delivered behind everything that enters our Spirit through our "eyes" threshold.

As wives, we have to find that place in God that would allow us to be help meets. It is not the husband, but because "you" NEVER said anything was wrong; he is not going to guess when something is wrong with you. We need to learn how to communicate. Sometimes, we feel that he should have known because he is our husband. But when your husband asks your opinion and you tell them, it does not matter even though it does matter, they are thinking everything is ok because we failed to communicate our true feeling about a matter or situation. Some of us have gone for years doing this same thing because we thought that is what we were supposed to do. Your mom did it that way; we feel it will work for us (news flash, you are not living in the same generation as your mom). You see the things that your mom experience, but you decided to do it the way your mom did it anyway. Your husband express that his father, his father's father did thing a certain way, and that is how he is going to run his household. We are not talking about God's foundational principles. We are talking about traditions such as the woman staying home and taking care of the house and the children, etc., and the men work to supply the needs of his household. MEN AND WOMEN ARE NOT WIRED THE SAME. Women get married and lose themselves into their family.

I Corinthians 7:34 it says: *the married women cares for the things of this world, how she can please her husband.*

How many of us really consider the Father and His Word as we prepare for Mr. or Mrs. Right. For example, you decided you see the quality of your future husband, all the signs were there while you were dating. You decided to take a chance at it, now you are in the marriage and you have lost yourself in having kids. Now the kids are grown and you are trying to figure out how did you get to the place you are at. Yes, we all change, situations, babies, careers and God requires that we change, but take a look at yourself first, because a lot of times as women, we feel like we can change our men. We feel like we can nurture anything back to health and in many instances, that is not the case. So before you decide to make a drastic change, take a look at you, have some communion with the Father, so He can give you direction. Usually, our mates have been who they are since we married them, and we are the ones that wake up some 5, 10 or even 15 years later realizing that we are not satisfied. The children are big enough to do for themselves, we no longer have to do "this" or "that." Now it is just you and your spouse and you are trying to figure out "what in the world has happened" to our romance, it has been years since any effort has been put into your romance. Try a date night, pillow talk, dinner, movies, walk in the park etc. anything and everything, start on common ground where both of you agree, so both of you can get the most out of your romance. This would eliminate one spouse feeling satisfied and the other feeling unsatisfied. Communication would allow both of you to learn to compromise and agree. It is not about one person but two people learning how to understand, communicate, nurture and nourish one another. Again, have some time with the Father, and allow Him to direct you. Nothing we get into happened overnight, so trust me, even you have changed. Therefore, you are going to have to sit down and communicate. One of the most tragic things, is that we feel like we can just express how we feel and our spouses will take it the way we saying it, from our perspective when they have no background information regarding that specific situation. This is when the Holy Spirit comes into play and God can give you the wisdom on the "how" and "when" to share. Sharing our place can be just as detrimental as you going off on a tangent and saying what you feeling like saying with no filters from the other person's point of view. We are supposed to be our husband's helpmeet according to the Word of God.

Ephesians 5:20-33 *Giving thanks always for all things unto God and the Father in the name of our Lord Jesus Christ; submitting yourselves one to another in the fear of God. Wives, submit yourselves unto your own husbands, as unto the Lord. For the husband is the head of the wife, even as Christ is the head of the church: and he is the Savior of the body.*

Therefore as the church is subject unto Christ, so let the wives be to their own husbands in everything. Husbands, love your wives, even as Christ also loved the church, and gave himself for it; That he might sanctify and cleanse it with the washing of water by the word, That he might present it to himself a glorious church, not having spot, or wrinkle, or any such thing; but that it should be holy and without blemish. So ought men to love their wives as their own bodies. He that loveth his wife loveth himself. For no man ever yet hated his own flesh; but nourisheth and cherisheth it, even as the Lord the church: For we are members of his body, of his flesh, and of his bones. For this cause shall a man leave his father and mother, and shall be joined unto his wife, and they two shall be one flesh. This is a great mystery: but I speak concerning Christ and the church. Nevertheless let every one of you in particular so love his wife even as himself; and the wife see that she reverence her husband.

ADDITIONAL SCRIPTURES:
I Corinthians 7
II Corinthians 6:14-18

Because of circumstances, we let everything go, our looks, our ambitions, goals and our relationship with our Heavenly Father. We "awake" after years of this repeated cycle and expect things to change because we find ourselves unhappy. This is when you get yourself together and ask God for guidance. II

Corinthians 6:14-18: *Do not be yoked together with unbelievers. For what do righteousness and wickedness have in*

common? Or what fellowship can light have with darkness? What harmony is there between Christ and Belial? Or what does a believer have in common with an unbeliever? What agreement is there between the temple of God and idols? For we are the temple of the living God. As God has said: "I will live with them and walk among them, and I will be their God, and they will be my people." Therefore, Come out from them and be separate, says the Lord. Touch no unclean thing, and I will receive you. And, "I will be a Father to you, and you will be my sons and daughters, says the Lord Almighty.

God has design the role of the husband and the wives, and we need to respect the Word of God and know that we do not know best, but God does.

Proverbs 14: 1-3 *The wise woman builds her house, but with her own hands the foolish one tears hers down. Whoever fears the Lord walks uprightly, but those who despise him are devious in their ways. A fool's mouth lashes out with pride, but the lips of the wise protect them.*

We have to be convinced that God knows us and he know the exact number of hairs on our head. If he knows that, we can agree that He does pay attention to the details of our lives.

Ephesians 5: 21-33 says: *Submit to one another out of reverence for Christ. Wives, submit yourselves to your own husbands as you do to the Lord. For the husband is the head of the wife as Christ is the head of the church, his body, of which he is the Savior. Now as the church submits to Christ, so also wives should submit to their husbands in everything. Husbands, love your wives, just as Christ loved the church and gave himself up for her to make her holy, cleansing her by the washing with water through the word, and to present her to himself as a radiant church, without stain or wrinkle or any other blemish, but holy and blameless. In this same way, husbands ought to love their wives as their own bodies. He who loves his wife loves himself. After all, no one ever hated their own body, but they feed and care for their body, just as Christ does the church—for we are members of his body "For this reason a man will leave his father and mother and be united to his wife, and the two will become one flesh.*

This is a profound mystery—but I am talking about Christ and the church. However, each one of you also must love his wife as he loves himself, and the wife must respect her husband.

As wives, in most instances, we set the tone for household and our husbands set the tone for the family and the order of God for his house. We have to treasure the Word of God and know that God has already design the path for our lives. However, when we are not taught or not reared in the Word of God, then we have to come into the knowledge of God and His Word and "submit" to the Word even when we do not understand. The longer it takes for us (women and men) to allow God to mold us into the people He designed before the foundation of the world; the longer it will take for each of us to understand and operate in our role according to the Word of God.

BODY

I AM SCREAMING BECAUSE I have done everything that I was big enough to do such as steal, murdered, drugs, pimp, prostitute, disrespectful to parents, hateful, hit people (i.e. spouse) slander, and prejudice—hateful toward other races, high minded, can I still go to Heaven? Yes, if you ask for forgiveness and accept Jesus as Lord. The Scripture talks about how Peter felt that the Gentiles are unclean; the Lord told him not to call unclean what God calls clean. The Scripture Act 10: 34-35 says: Then Peter began to speak: "I now realize how true it is that God does not show favoritism but accepts from every nation the one who fears him and does what is right.

To know that my Father does not have favorites like our earthly father should give all of us hope in Christ. Since our Heavenly Father does not have favorites, it does not matter what side of the "tracks" we come from; we all can receive the gift of salvation. God loves us with unprecedented love, no one will ever be able to love us like our Father in Heaven nor show mercy toward us like He does.

Furthermore, **St. Matthew 12: 30-37** says:
"Whoever is not with me is against me, and whoever does not

gather with me scatters. And so I tell you, every kind of sin and slander can be forgiven, but blasphemy against the Spirit will not be forgiven. Anyone who speaks a word against the Son of Man will be forgiven, but anyone who speaks against the Holy Spirit will not be forgiven, either in this age or in the age to come. Make a tree good and its fruit will be good, or make a tree bad and its fruit will be bad, for a tree is recognized by its fruit. You brood of vipers, how can you who are evil say anything good? For the mouth speaks what the heart is full of. A good man brings good things out of the good stored up in him, and an evil man brings evil things out of the evil stored up in him. But I tell you that everyone will have to give account on the Day of Judgment for every empty word they have spoken. For by your words you will be acquitted, and by your words you will be condemned."

This Scripture reminds us that there is no sin that we will not be forgiven except those who speak against the Holy Spirit. Again, the roadmap is the Scripture, which shows us how to win in every part of our lives. The only thing we need to do is walk in the way the Father has given us along with allowing the Holy Spirit to guide us unto all truths. John 16:13 says: But when he, the Spirit of truth, comes, he will guide you into all the truth. He will not speak on his own; he will speak only what he hears, and he will tell you what is yet to come.

I John 3:16-24 says: *This is how we know what love is: Jesus Christ laid down his life for us. And we ought to lay* *down our lives for our brothers and sisters. If anyone has material possessions and sees a brother or sister in need but has no pity on them, how can the love of God be in that person? Dear children, let us not love with words or speech but with actions and in truth. This is how we know that we belong to the truth and how we set our hearts at rest in his presence: If our hearts condemn us, we know that God is greater than our hearts, and he knows everything. Dear friends, if our hearts do not condemn us, we have confidence before God and receive from him anything we ask, because we keep his commands and do what pleases him. And this is his command: to believe in the name of his Son, Jesus Christ, and to love one another as he commanded us. The one who keeps God's commands lives in him, and he in them. And this is how we know that he lives in us: We know it by the Spirit he gave us.*

This should remind us that we do not have to be from a certain family or be in a certain income bracket in order to accept Jesus as Lord and Savior of our lives. If truth be told, when people have all they need, they feel there's no need for Jesus. However, salvation is not something that we can buy or sell, it is solely about acceptance of the gift of salvation from our Lord and Savior. Also, we cannot work our way into Heaven. God has a purpose for our lives, He has given us the instructions for the "good life" through the Word of God.

Jeremiah 29: 10-14 says: *This is what the Lord says: "When seventy years are completed for Babylon, I will come to* *you and fulfill my good promise to bring you back to this place. For I know the plans I have for you," declares the Lord, "plans to prosper you and not to harm you, plans to give you hope and a future. Then you will call on me and come and pray to me, and I will listen to you. You will seek me and find me when you seek me with all your heart. I will be found by you," declares the Lord, "and will bring you back from captivity.*

Additionally, God reminds us of His love and concern for us because in **Psalm 37:37-40**

Consider the blameless, observe the upright; a future awaits those who seek peace. But all sinners will be destroyed; there will be no future for the wicked. The salvation of the righteous comes from the Lord; he is their stronghold in time of trouble. The Lord helps them and delivers them; he delivers them from the wicked and saves them, because they take refuge in him.

I AM SCREAMING BECAUSE I am not a Christian; *per say* I am an atheist, Catholic, Lutheran, Muslim. Am I going to hell if I do not accept Jesus as Lord and Savior (none get to the father except by the son)?

Romans 10:9 says: *That if thou shalt confess with thy mouth the Lord Jesus, and shalt believe in thine heart that God hath raised him from the dead, thou shalt be saved.*

This lets us know that there is no color barrier to the kingdom, just confession of the mouth. It does not matter what religion you are; it is a blessing that you found the way to the Father before you leave this earth. Sometimes we feel like we are not worth it because we have not been saved that long, but living in Christ is a lifestyle with the Holy Spirit guiding us into all truths.

John 14: 6-7 says: *Jesus saith unto him, I am the way, the truth, and the life: no man cometh unto the Father, but by me. If ye had known me, ye should have known my Father also: and from henceforth ye know him, and have seen him.*

This is a reminder that it does not matter where we come from, what our background is or what we've confessed before, now is the appointed time (when we come into the knowledge of God).

John 3:5 says: *Jesus answered, Verily, verily, I say unto thee, except a man be born of water and of the Spirit, he cannot enter into the kingdom of God.*

ADDITIONAL SCRIPTURES:
Psalm 63:5
Proverbs 31:26
Psalm 89:1
Psalm 71:8
Acts 10:34

I AM SCREAMING BECAUSE I work with people who say they are Christians (black, white, etc.) but they talk about me just as the unsaved do.

Matthew 5:16 says: *Let your light so shine before men, that they may see your good works, and glorify your Father which is in Heaven.*

Much of our lives, we have learned how to become people pleasers, but when we get the revelation about who our Father really is; our standards will be raised and people will be wondering why are we so different. If we develop our relationship with the Father; He will help us in each situation. We will have to learn how to let our light shine in the workplace as a witness to the light that is within us. We as humans feel like we are justified if we do *tit for tack* to those who wrong us, and if we are thinking like that our relationship is not developed in God.

Ephesians 6:14 says: *Stand therefore, having your loins girt about with truth, and having on the breastplate of righteousness.*

We have to keep our eyes fixed on Jesus and His perfect example because He is our advocate, and understands that we are only justified in Jesus.

2 Corinthians 4:4 says: *In whom the god of this world hath blinded the minds of them which believe not, lest the light of the glorious gospel of Christ, who is the image of God, should shine unto them.*

All of us were not raised in a Christian home, but our parents did the best they could with what they knew. When we are not taught how to stand Spiritually, it will cause us to fight in the Spirit at first. Once we start standing on the Word of God consistently; we start to see a transformation in our own lives, and in our life situations we go through. We have to learn how to rejoice and see that God is working our situation out in our favor because we are walking by the Word of God.

ADDITIONAL SCRIPTURES
Psalm 40:1
Psalm 37:34
Psalm 33:20
Psalm 1:5
Psalm 39:7
Psalm 7:9
Psalm 27:14
2 Thessalonians 2:15

BODY
I AM SCREAMING BECAUSE I am gay, homosexual and I do not know how to get out of this life.

Romans 1:27 *And likewise also the men, leaving the natural use of the woman, burned in their lust one toward another;*

men with men working that which is unseemly, and receiving in themselves that recompense of their error which was meet.

Roman 1:18-27 says*: The wrath of God is being revealed from Heaven against all the godlessness and wickedness of people, who suppress the truth by their wickedness, since what may be known about God is plain to them, because God has made it plain to them. For since the creation of the world God's invisible qualities—his eternal power and divine nature—have been clearly seen, being understood from what has been made, so that people are without excuse. For although they knew God, they neither glorified him as God nor gave thanks to him, but their thinking became futile and their foolish hearts were darkened. Although they claimed to be wise, they became fools and exchanged the glory of the immortal God for images made to look like a mortal human being and birds and animals and reptiles. Therefore God gave them over in the sinful desires of their hearts to sexual impurity for the degrading of their bodies with one another. They exchanged the truth about God for a lie, and worshiped and served created things rather than the Creator—who is forever praised. Amen. Because of this, God gave them over to shameful lusts. Even their women exchanged natural sexual relations for unnatural ones. In the same way the men also abandoned natural relations with women and were inflamed with lust for one another. Men committed shameful acts with other men, and received in themselves the due penalty for their error.*

You feel like no one understands how you feel, but we all get thoughts that are contrary to our way of life, however, we cannot let that thought take root in the mind and spirit because if we do, we will act on that thought. A thought is just a thought until we take action to it. What do you mean? I mean that thoughts come, we either entertain them or ignore them. In addition, if we rehearse a thought continually, that one thought; at some point; whether positively or negatively will find something to latch onto inside of us. Perhaps it was a thought you had; something your parents said, or something the person you value the most have mentioned more than a couple of times. That one thought has taken up so much of your thought pattern that when it does move from a thought to the state of manifestation, you do not know when or how. Immediately, when thoughts come in because of the will of God, we have the power to cast those thoughts down out of our minds and lives. There is power in our words and we have to believe that as we speak the Word of God, the angels excel in strength to perform the Word of God. Understand that this battle is Spiritual.

II Corinthians 10:4 says: *The weapons we fight with are not the weapons of the world. On the contrary, they have divine power to demolish strongholds.*

If I have never been in your shoes, or unless the Holy Spirit gives a revelatory knowledge to a person, they will not know about your situation in order to help you if you are expecting help.

On the contrary, if someone tries to minister to you and your mind and spirit are closed; they might as well not minister because you are not in a position to receive what has been sent to you through that person anyway. The Word of God tells us to *renew our minds daily*, and He has given us the blueprint of success which is the Word of God. Any and every answer that we need is in the Word.

There is nothing new under the sun, and we have to take responsibility for our actions and our thoughts. The Word of God tells us to *bring everything that exalts itself against the knowledge of God under subjection.* **Romans 12:2** *And be not conformed to this world: but be ye transformed by the renewing of your mind, that ye may prove what is that good, and acceptable, and perfect, will of God.*

ADDITIONAL SCRIPTURES
James 1:23
1 Corinthians 2:14
Ephesians 4:23
Romans 12:16
Colossians 1:21
Psalm 51:10

MIND

I AM SCREAMING BECAUSE I am Asian, Black, Hispanic, Indian, or White and I do not like other ethnic races. Am I going to hell?

Romans 7: 5-24 says: *For when we were in the flesh, the motions of sins, which were by the law, did work in our members to bring forth fruit unto death. But now we are* *delivered from the law, that being dead wherein we were held; that we should serve in newness of Spirit, and not in the oldness of the letter. What shall we say then? Is the law sin? God forbid. Nay, I had not known sin, but by the law: for I had not known lust, except the law had said, Thou shalt not covet. But sin, taking occasion by the commandment, wrought in me all manner of concupiscence. For without the law sin was dead.*

For I was alive without the law once: but when the commandment came, sin revived, and I died. And the commandment, which was ordained to life, I found to be unto death. For sin, taking occasion by the commandment, deceived me, and by it slew me. Wherefore the law is holy, and the commandment holy, and just, and good. Was then that which is good made death unto me? God forbid. But sin, that it might appear sin, working death in me by that which is good; that sin by the commandment might become exceeding sinful. For we know that the law is Spiritual: but I am carnal, sold under sin.

For that which I do I allow not: for what I would, that do I not; but what I hate, that do I. If then I do that which I would not, I consent unto the law that it is good. Now then it is no more I that do it, but sin that dwelleth in me. For I know that in me (that is, in my flesh,) dwelleth no good thing: for to will is present with me; but how to perform that which is good I find not. For the good that I would I do not: but the evil which I would not, that I do. Now if I do that I would not, it is no more I that do it, but sin that dwelleth in me. I find then a law, that, when I would do good, evil is present with me. For I delight in the law of God after the inward man: But I see another law in my members, warring against the law of my mind, and bringing me into captivity to the law of sin which is in my members. O wretched man that I am! Who shall deliver me from the body of this death? I thank God through Jesus Christ our Lord. So then with the mind I myself serve the law of God; but with the flesh the law of sin.

In our flesh, there is nothing but sin because we are born into a world of sin. The only way we can get to the Father is through the Son. We cannot save or deliver ourselves; we have to accept Jesus as our Lord and Savior and allow the Word of God to help shape our lives into what God has ordained from the foundation of the world. Again, it does not matter what we have done, if we accept Jesus as Lord, we shall be saved. **Acts 10:34** says: *Then Peter opened his mouth, and said, of a truth I perceive that God is no respecter of persons.*

BODY

I AM SCREAMING BECAUSE I have been molested and I cannot get this out of my mind. I am plagued by my circumstances.

Romans 12: 1-3 says: *I beseech you therefore, brethren, by the mercies of God, that ye present your bodies a living sacrifice, holy, acceptable unto God, which is your reasonable service. And be not conformed to this world: but be ye transformed by the renewing of your mind, that ye may prove what is that good, and acceptable, and perfect, will of God. For I say, through the grace given unto me, to every man that is among you, not to think of himself more highly than he ought to* *think; but to think soberly, according as God hath dealt to every man the measure of faith.*

As we read **Roman 7**, we learn our flesh fights against our Spirit. As we begin to feed our spirit by reading the Word of God, we begin to develop our personal relationship with our personal Savior, Jesus. Through the Word of God, we will know that we have to renew our minds daily, stay on our knees, and keep our minds on Christ. God never said that we would not think things outside of His Will, but we have to go boldly to the throne of grace and ask for forgiveness for our sins and offenses against God and our brothers and sisters.

When we go through a thing; it can sometimes be very hard because of the constant fight between the flesh and Spirit. God is able to get us through any situation if we keep our minds stayed on him.

Isaiah 26:3 says: *Thou wilt keep him in perfect peace, whose mind is stayed on thee: because he trusteth in thee.*

We have to CHOOSE to trust the Word of God and apply the Word of God to our situations. Faith is an action word and we have to work (apply) the Word of God, and it will work for us.

Once we get through certain situations, we cannot continue rehearsing the incident because it makes us mad all over again. If we pay attention to the Word of

God, it tells us what our flesh is made of.

Romans 7:25 says: *I thank God through Jesus Christ our Lord. So then with the mind I myself serve the law of God; but with the flesh the law of sin.*

God is the one who made us, and He has designed the perfect plan for our lives and a way of escape when we find ourselves outside of the will of God.

Philippians 4:7 says: *And the peace of God, which passeth all understanding, shall keep your hearts and minds through Christ Jesus.*

This is the protection that we need to live victorious here on this earth. The battleground is in our mind. We can dress up the natural man; however, we have to allow the Holy Spirit to guide us to all truths through the Word. Learning what His plan for us through reading the Word, praying, fasting and meditating, will allow us to avoid the enemy's snares. This helps us to further develop our relationship with our personal Savior, Jesus.

ADDITIONAL SCRIPTURES:
Romans 15:6
Roman 7:14-25
1 Corinthians 1:10
Ephesians 2:3

MIND

I AM SCREAMING BECAUSE I am not a good person, parent, worker, saint, and I know it, but I cannot seem to change it.

Roman 7:14-25 says: *For we know that the law is Spiritual: but I am carnal, sold under sin. For that which I do I allow not: for what I would, that do I not; but what I hate, that do I. If then I do that which I would not, I consent unto the law that it is good. Now then it is no more I that do it, but sin that dwelleth in me. For I know that in me (that is, in my flesh,) dwelleth no good thing: for to will is present with me; but how to perform that which is good I find not. For the good that I would I do not: but the evil which I would not, that I do. Now if I do that I would not, it is no more I that do it, but sin that dwelleth in me. I find then a law, that, when I would do good, evil is present with me. For I delight in the law of God after the inward man: But I see another law in my members, warring against the law of my mind, and bringing me into captivity to the law of sin which is in my members. O wretched man that I am! Who shall deliver me from the body of this death? I thank God through Jesus Christ our Lord. So then with the mind I myself serve the law of God; but with the flesh the law of sin.*

There is nothing we can say to the Holy Spirit He does not already know. The Word of God teaches the *Holy Spirit will guide us unto all truths.* So when we are trying to deceive God, we are really deceiving ourselves and are out of touch with our own "truth."

Jesus is the only person that will not judge us in our situation, and have mercy on us even when we deserve what we are going through. He is such a loving Father, Redeemer, Savior and Friend. The Father hath need of thee! Won't you answer Him? Surely, as you are doing His Will; be assured that He is working things out in your favor.

I AM SCREAMING BECAUSE I want to do better but do not know how. We sometimes think that we can control our own selves. Yes, we can if the Holy Spirit is directing us and is our keeper. However, in our own selves, there is nothing that we can do.

Romans 8 says: *There is therefore now no condemnation to them which are in Christ Jesus, who walk not after the flesh, but after the Spirit. For the law of the Spirit of life in Christ Jesus hath made me free from the law of sin and death. For what the law could not do, in that it was weak through the flesh, God sending his own Son in the likeness of sinful flesh, and for sin, condemned sin in the flesh: That the righteousness of the law might be fulfilled in us, who walk not after the flesh, but after the Spirit. For they that are after the flesh do mind the things of the flesh; but they that are after the Spirit the things of the Spirit. For to be carnally minded is death; but to be Spiritually minded is life and peace. Because the carnal mind is enmity against God: for it is not subject to the law of God, neither indeed can be. So then they that are in the flesh cannot please God. But ye are not in the flesh, but in the*

Spirit, if so be that the Spirit of God dwell in you. Now if any man have not the Spirit of Christ, he is none of his. And if Christ be in you, the body is dead because of sin; but the Spirit is life because of righteousness. But if the Spirit of him that raised up Jesus from the dead dwell in you, he that raised up Christ from the dead shall also quicken your mortal bodies by his Spirit that dwelleth in you. Therefore, brethren, we are debtors, not to the flesh, to live after the flesh. For if ye live after the flesh, ye shall die: but if ye through the Spirit do mortify the deeds of the body, ye shall live. For as many as are led by the Spirit of God, they are the sons of God. For ye have not received the Spirit of bondage again to fear; but ye have received the Spirit of adoption, whereby we cry, Abba, Father. The Spirit itself beareth witness with our Spirit, that we are the children of God: And if children, then heirs; heirs of God, and joint-heirs with Christ; if so be that we suffer with him, that we may be also glorified together. For I reckon that the sufferings of this present time are not worthy to be compared with the glory which shall be revealed in us. For the earnest expectation of the creature waiteth for the manifestation of the sons of God. For the creature was made subject to vanity, not willingly, but by reason of him who hath subjected the same in hope, Because the creature itself also shall be delivered from the bondage of corruption into the glorious liberty of the children of God. For we know that the whole creation groaneth and travaileth in pain together until now. And not only they, but ourselves also, which have the firstfruits of the Spirit, even we ourselves groan within ourselves, waiting for the adoption, to wit, the redemption of our body. For we are saved by hope: but hope that is seen is not hope: for what a man seeth, why doth he yet hope for? But if we hope for that we see not, then do we with patience wait for it.

We do not have to know everything, but know the Holy Spirit is leading us. We cannot know unless we search the Word of God and know what the Word says about our lives and our situations.

Some are feeling so alone, but know that's what the enemy wants you to think. The ultimate goal of the enemy is to kill, steal, rob and destroy. The devil does not want us to realize who we are in Christ or whose we are once we accept Jesus into our hearts as our Lord and Savior.

Many people confess Jesus, but do not let Him become Lord over their lives. We start off doing what the Word of God tells us, but sometimes we get off course because of our choices or the issues of life which distract us from the Will of God. We are good people, but being good does not get our names written in the Lamb's Book of Life. He asked His disciples a question which was *Why do you call me Lord and do not what I say* **Luke 6:46**. What good is it for us to have the map of life but do not use it in life. We all are free moral agents and we have to choose to do what the Word of God says, but we choose not to do it God's way. Know there are consequences for choosing to do life your own way. Some people are never able to get back to their place of peace because of their choices.

ADDITIONAL SCRIPTURES:
Psalms 34
Psalms 51
Romans 7
Romans 8

BODY

I AM SCREAMING BECAUSE the people that I hang around with do not like me and I know it, but I keep hanging with them anyway.

Roman 7:14-25 says: *For we know that the law is Spiritual: but I am carnal, sold under sin. For that which I do I allow not: for what I would, that do I not; but what I hate, that do I. If then I do that which I would not, I consent unto the law that it is good. Now then it is no more I that do it, but sin that dwelleth in me. For I know that in me (that is, in my flesh,) dwelleth no good thing: for to will is present with me; but how to perform that which is good I find not. For the good that I would I do not: but the evil which I would not, that I do. Now if I do that I would not, it is no more I that do it, but sin that dwelleth in me. I find then a law, that, when I would do good, evil is present with me. For I delight in the law of God after the inward man: But I see another law in my members, warring against the law of my mind, and bringing me into captivity to the law of sin which is in my members. O wretched man that I am! Who shall deliver me from the body of this death? I thank God through Jesus Christ our Lord. So then* *with the mind I myself serve the law of God; but with the flesh the law of sin.*

No one knows the Spirit of a man but that man;

1 Corinthians 2:11 which says: *For what man knoweth the things of a man, save the Spirit of man which is in him? Even so the things of God knoweth no man, but the Spirit of God.*

No two can walk together unless they agree. This means that if we do not agree with the things that is being done; then we will disagree and possibly stop being friends. Therefore, what we believe and how we were raised causes us to choose things that are harmful to us and our walk with God. Choosing things opposite of what God says will threaten our relationship with our Savior.

I AM SCREAMING BECAUSE I am living with this man/woman and now it has been years and I do not think I am going to be married.

Proverbs 31 says: *The words of king Lemuel, the prophecy that his mother taught him. What, my son? And what, the son of my womb? And what, the son of my vows? Give not thy strength unto women, nor thy ways to that which destroyeth kings. It is not for kings, O Lemuel, it is not for kings to drink wine; nor for princes strong drink: Lest they drink, and forget the law, and pervert the judgment of any of* *the afflicted. Give strong drink unto him that is ready to perish, and wine unto those that be of heavy hearts. Let him drink, and forget his poverty, and remember his misery no more. Open thy mouth for the dumb in the cause of all such as are appointed to destruction. Open thy mouth, judge righteously, and plead the cause of the poor and needy. Who can find a virtuous woman? For her price is far above rubies. The heart of her husband doth safely trust in her, so that he shall have no need of spoil. She will do him good and not evil all the days of her life. She seeketh wool, and flax, and worketh willingly with her hands. She is like the merchants' ships; she bringeth her food from afar. She riseth also while it is yet night, and giveth meat to her household, and a portion to her maidens. She considereth a field, and buyeth it: with the fruit of her hands she planteth a vineyard. She girdeth her loins with strength, and strengtheneth her arms. She perceiveth that her merchandise is good: her candle goeth not out by night. She layeth her hands to the spindle, and her hands hold the distaff. She stretcheth out her hand to the poor; yea, she reacheth forth her hands to the needy. She is not afraid of the snow for her household: for all her household are clothed with scarlet. She maketh herself coverings of tapestry; her clothing is silk and purple. Her husband is known in the gates, when he sitteth among the elders of the land. She maketh fine linen, and selleth it; and delivereth girdles unto the merchant. Strength and honour are her clothing; and she shall rejoice in time to come. She openeth her mouth with wisdom; and in her tongue is the law of kindness. She looketh well to the ways of her household, and eateth not the bread of idleness. Her children arise up, and call her blessed; her husband also, and he praiseth her. Many daughters have done virtuously, but thou excellest them all. Favour is deceitful, and beauty is vain: but a woman that feareth the LORD, she shall be praised. Give her of the fruit of her hands; and let her own works praise her in the gates.*

The media feeds so many things in our spirits. We see so much as children in school and in our adult lives. Seeing all these things with our natural eyes can make us question what the Father in Heaven says about us. This is why it is so important to allow Jesus to be Lord over our lives.

We have to teach our children the ways of the Lord because the enemy and the world's way is enmity against God. As we train our children, we get them to buy into what the Word of God says and use every opportunity to train them in the things of the Lord (using the Bible as our teaching book). We cannot get so focus on us and what we want that we forget about our responsibility that God has given to us as parents, mothers, fathers, sisters, brothers, teachers, mentors, etc.

As women, we need to know that we are the ones who are waiting and being pursued by the man that God has designed for us, not the other way around. If we listen to society's message we will seek for our mate, but do what the Bible says. Stop trying to help God out because God has good thoughts concerning us. Stop looking or seeking from your emotions, (carnal man).

Romans 8:6-7 says: *For to be carnally minded is death; but to be Spiritually minded is life and peace. Because the carnal mind is enmity against God: for it is not subject to the law of God, neither indeed can be.*

It is amazing to me that God created the world and designed a plan for our lives to WIN in each and every situation. He is not saying that we will not go through anything, He just assured us that He has designed a way of escape. The Scripture says that *no one can perceive the thing of the Spirit save the Spirit of a man.* We feel we are doing God a favor by putting our "stakes" into "him/her" (the person we feel should be our spouse) before someone else does because "they are a good person." The choice is not necessarily based on what the Word of God says, but based on our fleshly desires.

ADDITIONAL SCRIPTURES:
Ephesians 5
I Corinthians 7
Romans 7
Romans 8

I AM SCREAMING BECAUSE I cannot forgive my mother, father, sister, brother, aunt, uncle, cousin, supervisor (boss) for what they did to me.

The Word of God says that *if we regard iniquity in our hearts the Lord cannot hear us.* The sin separates us from the presence of God. In addition, unforgiveness means you are holding on to what that person has done to you and therefore, you cannot move forward.

Matthew 6:15 says: *But if ye forgive not men their trespasses, neither will your Father forgive your trespasses.*

How is that we always want people to forgive us, but when it is time for us to forgive, it is truly harder. The Word of God tells us to use the same measure to measure that which is measured to us. So if we are forgiven, then it should be easier for us to forgive if we are communing with the Father.

In the Old Testament passage
1 Kings 8:36 says: *Then hear thou in Heaven, and forgive the sin of thy servants, and of thy people Israel, that thou teach them the good way wherein they should walk, and give rain upon thy land, which thou hast given to thy people for an inheritance.*

We have to make sure our affections are on the things above and not on earthly things.

Colossians 3 says: *If ye then be risen with Christ, seek those things which are above, where Christ sitteth on the right hand of God. Set your affection on things above, not on things on the earth. For ye are dead, and your life is hid with Christ* *in God. When Christ, who is our life, shall appear, then shall ye also appear with him in glory? Mortify therefore your members which are upon the earth; fornication, uncleanness, inordinate affection, evil concupiscence, and covetousness, which is idolatry: For which things' sake the wrath of God cometh on the children of disobedience: In the which ye also walked some time, when ye lived in them. But now ye also put off all these; anger, wrath, malice, blasphemy, filthy communication out of your mouth. Lie not one to another, seeing that ye have put off the old man with his deeds; And have put on the new man, which is renewed in knowledge after the image of him that created him: Where there is neither Greek nor Jew, circumcision nor uncircumcision, Barbarian, Scythian, bond nor free: but Christ is all, and in all. Put on therefore, as the elect of God, holy and beloved, bowels of mercies, kindness, humbleness of mind, meekness, longsuffering; forbearing one another, and forgiving one another, if any man have a quarrel against any: even as Christ forgave you, so also do ye. And above all these things put on charity, which is the bond of perfectness. And let the peace of God rule in your hearts, to which also ye are called in one body; and be ye thankful. Let the word of Christ dwell in you richly in all wisdom; teaching and admonishing one another in psalms and hymns and Spiritual songs, singing with grace in your hearts to the Lord. And whatsoever ye do in word or deed, do all in the name of the Lord Jesus, giving thanks to God and the Father by him. Wives, submit yourselves unto your own husbands, as it is fit in the Lord. Husbands, love your wives, and be not bitter against them. Children, obey your parents in all things: for this is well pleasing unto the Lord. Fathers, provoke not your children to anger, lest they be discouraged. Servants, obey in all things your masters according to the flesh; not with eyeservice, as men pleasers; but in singleness of heart, fearing God; And whatsoever ye do, do it heartily, as to the Lord, and not unto men; Knowing that of the Lord ye shall receive the reward of the inheritance: for ye serve the Lord Christ. But he that doeth wrong shall receive for the wrong which he hath done: and there is no respect of persons.*

If we cannot forgive, it has such an impact on our mind. We are constantly rehearsing the "act" of what was done and therefore we cannot focus on anything else. Before you know it, months and years have passed and it seems like you are the only one who has not moved on. It takes the Love of God to deal with some people and something that has happened to us so we can move forward. If we are stuck in unforgiveness, then spiritually we are at a stagnant place because we have not allowed God to help us through the situation. We say "God I give this problem or situation to you" but we have that thing on our minds, constantly. This is not giving it to God. Even when we give it to God, that does not mean that we will not think about it from time to time, but it does mean that we will not get stuck on what happened because the blood of Jesus covers all our sins. Unforgiveness has an impact on us naturally, emotionally and Spiritually, and it brings bitterness which kills us from the inside to the outside. Is there help for us? The answer is yes, first forgive yourself and give yourself time in the repentance stage, grieve, it is alright. Then get up, dust yourself off and move on. How? By the Word of God and spending time in fellowship with the Father. Our situation does have an impact on our destiny.

ADDITIONAL SCRIPTURES:
Acts 26:17-18
Ephesians 4:31
II Timothy 3:1-7
Ephesians 4:22-24
Acts 8:23
Matthew 18:21-35

I AM SCREAMING BECAUSE GOD does not hold the deepest place in my heart.

My husband, job, children, houses, land, money, and cars do. How do I get God to His rightful place in my life? Nothing can change until we acknowledge and ask God to help us change. We are only passing through this earth, and the Bible tells us not to put our trust in earthly treasures. More explicitly put,

Matthew 6:19-20 says: *Lay not up for yourselves treasures upon earth, where moth and rust doth corrupt, and where thieves break through and steal: But lay up for yourselves treasures in Heaven, where neither moth nor rust doth corrupt, and where thieves do not break through nor steal.*

This is a daily walk with God and the Holy Ghost will lead us unto all truths. Again, we are free moral agents and even if we know the Word of God, we have to choose to obey or not to obey. Some people are chosen to do certain things for the Kingdom of God. Sometimes we hear people say that they ran, doing everything they were big enough to do, but one day came to a breaking point. They realized that they needed Jesus; they accepted Jesus and has never looked back at their life with any regret. They made a decision for God to be Lord of their lives and the Holy Spirit to guide them unto all truths. No one ever said that it would be easy, but in the Word of God, He lets us know that we will have a way of escape. The Holy Spirit is still your helper, if you let Him.

SPIRIT

I AM SCREAMING BECAUSE the enemy never wants us to realize the purpose God has for any of us or the fulfillment that comes with a relationship.

> **Psalm 16:11** says: *Thou wilt shew me the path of life: in thy presence is fullness of joy; at thy right hand there are pleasures for evermore.*

Another Scripture showing us the blessings of the Lord is

Psalm 23:5 says: *Thou preparest a table before me in the presence of mine enemies: thou anointest my head with oil; my cup runneth over.*

Additionally, **Psalm 140:13** says: *Surely the righteous shall give thanks unto thy name: the upright shall dwell in thy presence.*

There is hope in Christ.

In **Galatians 5:1** says: *Stand fast therefore in the liberty wherewith Christ hath made us free, and be not entangled again with the yoke of bondage.*

Ultimately, if we don't allow God to be head of our lives, we will never reach our full potential or live a victorious life on earth. A yoke of bondage can be anything that keeps us from the liberties of Christ; such as our own selves, spouse, children, job, past, and anxiousness. The Word of God is filled with promises, but the question is, do we really believe what the Scriptures says about our past? He will throw it behind His back. He wants to bring us to our expected end in Him.

Psalm 16:1 says: *Preserve me, O God: for in thee do I put my trust;* **8-11** says: *I have set the Lord always before me: because he is at my right hand, I shall not be moved. Therefore my heart is glad, and my glory rejoiceth: my flesh also shall rest in hope. For thou wilt not leave my soul in hell; neither wilt thou suffer thine Holy One to see corruption. Thou wilt shew* *me the path of life: in thy presence is fullness of joy; at thy right hand there are pleasures for evermore.*

We have to be reminded that just as God is working hard for His children; the enemy is working just as hard against us. According to the Word of God, the enemy's purpose is to kill, steal, rob and destroy.

1 Peter 5:8 says: *Be sober, be vigilant; because your adversary the devil, as a roaring lion, walketh about, and seeking whom he may devour.*

SPIRIT
I AM SCREAMING BECAUSE I do not know how to believe and let my gift work for me.

Isaiah 64:4-5 says: *For since the beginning of the world men have not heard, nor perceived by the ear, neither hath the eye seen, O God, beside thee, what he hath prepared for him that waiteth for him. Thou meetest him that rejoiceth and worketh righteousness, those that remember thee in thy ways.*

For some of us, it was not until after being saved a while that we started experiencing trials, began trusting God and believed His Word. The Scripture reminds us that God had us on His mind long before we had Him on our minds, Amen. Personally, we choose to remember the Words of the Lord regarding our lives. Sometimes we get so sidetracked into focusing on life issues, such as: children, spouses, jobs, material things, sickness, the things people do to us, getting them back because of what they have done to us; and spending time adjusting our lives.

We act as though we can protect ourselves better than Jesus can. It is not always the devil that causes things to happen in our lives. Some things are a result of the decisions we make with or without consulting the Father or seeking godly counsel, etc.

Traditionally we want people to endorse the gift given to us by God, and we get sidetracked when people do not respond the way we think they should respond. Is this our natural spirit talking? Sometimes, we can be so convinced of something because that is what we want so bad, we think it is coming from our Spirit man, but because we want that particular thing so bad we will it from our Spirit. If we are not asking or looking for God's guidance or direction, then we will not get it. He is no respecter of person, but He is not going to override our wills. We have to choose to seek out, and obey on purpose what the will of the Lord is. There is a Scripture that says, *"The fear of the Lord is the beginning of wisdom."*

Proverbs 18:15-16 says: *The heart of the prudent getteth knowledge; and the ear of the wise seeketh knowledge. A man's gift maketh room for him, and bringeth him before great men.*

Reading the Scripture help us stay focused on what our assignment is and keeps us in the presence of the Lord. Sometimes we can get sidetrack focusing on what we think and not what the Word of God says. There should be a confidence in our Father because all the things He has already done; He did them to ensure our success in Him.

1 John 4:10 says: *Herein is love, not that we loved God, but that he loved us, and sent his Son to be the propitiation for our sins.*

Again, this Scripture is confirmation of our Father's love for us. Salvation is a gift from God and we have to choose to accept that gift. Perception is reality for a person which means how we perceive a thing, for the most part is how it is in "our world." It takes the Word of God to straighten us out and keep us straighten out. We have to ask, "Lord help us to perceive ourselves as you see us, and keep us on the highway of holiness." Simply put, so we all can understand it.

1 John 3:1 says: *Behold, what manner of love the Father hath bestowed upon us, that we should be called the sons of God: therefore the world knoweth us not, because it knew him not.*

When we accept Jesus as Lord and Savior, we are

to take on His nature. The only way we can know His nature is by developing a personal relationship with Him through the Word of God. As we begin to spend time in His presence, we will begin to see things through the "eyes of the Word of God." We will not have to envy people and their gift because each one of us have our own gift from God. The Scripture reminds us of this and it says *one gift after this manner and another gift after that manner.*

People are sometimes envious because of a lack of development of the gift they have or do not take time to receive a revelation from God about the gift given through the Word of God. The Bible reminds us that *He chastens those He loves.*

ADDITIONAL SCRIPTURES:
I John 5:18
Romans 8
Colossians 3
Romans 7

SPIRIT

I AM SCREAMING BECAUSE I have never smoked, drank, fornicate, or committed adultery.

Will I still go to hell if I do not accept Jesus as Lord and Savior? The answer is yes; you will go to hell if you do not accept Jesus.

John 14:6 *Jesus saith unto him, I am the way, the truth, and the life: no man cometh unto the Father, but by me.*

We all have sinned and come short of the glory of God according to **Romans 3:23.** It goes further than us because **Romans 5:12** says: *Wherefore, as by one man sin entered into the world, and death by sin; and so death passed upon all men, for that all have sinned.*

We have to go to the throne daily to find help for us in our situations, and know that without Him we can do nothing.

Psalm 51 says: *Have mercy upon me, O God, according to thy lovingkindness: according unto the multitude of thy tender mercies blot out my transgressions. Wash me thoroughly from mine iniquity, and cleanse me from my sin. For I acknowledge my transgressions: and my sin is ever before me. Against thee, thee only, have I sinned, and done this evil in thy sight: that thou mightest be justified when thou speakest, and be clear when thou judgest. Behold, I was shapen in iniquity; and in sin did my mother conceive me. Behold, thou desirest truth in the inward parts: and in the hidden part thou shalt make me to know wisdom. Purge me with hyssop, and I shall be clean: wash me, and I shall be whiter than snow. Make me to hear joy and gladness; that the bones which thou hast broken may rejoice. Hide thy face from my sins, and blot out all mine iniquities. Create in me a clean heart, O God; and renew a right Spirit within me. Cast me not away from thy presence; and take not thy holy Spirit from me. Restore unto me the joy of thy salvation; and uphold me with thy free Spirit. Then will I teach transgressors thy ways; and sinners shall be converted unto thee. Deliver me from blood guiltiness, O God, thou God of my salvation: and my tongue shall sing aloud of thy righteousness. O Lord, open thou my lips; and my mouth shall shew forth thy praise. For thou desirest not sacrifice; else would I give it: thou delightest not in burnt offering.*

The sacrifices of God are a broken Spirit: *a broken and a contrite heart, O God, thou wilt not despise. Do good in thy good pleasure unto Zion: build thou the walls of Jerusalem. Then shalt thou be pleased with the sacrifices of righteousness, with burnt offering and whole burnt offering: then shall they offer bullocks upon thine altar.*

In this body, we do not have an advantage over the enemy unless we allow the Holy Spirit to operate in us according to Word of God. God desires to bless us with all spiritual blessings, but again, it is conditional. We must choose to do things differently from the Lord's standpoint. Otherwise, the Father's hands are tied because He is also bound by His own words. Be led by the Spirit and not by our natural/carnal man.

Remember, there is a constant battle between the flesh and Spirit. If we are operating in the Spirit, then the Spirit will rule our bodies. Subsequently, if we are operating in the natural, then our carnal man will rule. The Word of God tells us whatever we put into our Spirits will come out of our Spirit. Are you feeding your Spirit and starving your carnal man or are you feeding your carnal man and starving the carnal man? We are not talking about taking care of your natural body with the things we need in the natural to survive such as food, shelter, etc. We are talking about feeding your Spirit man the Word of God.

ADDITIONAL SCRIPTURES:
Romans 3:23
Romans 5:20
Romans 5:12

I AM SCREAMING BECAUSE I want to remain friends with my friends even though I know what you said Lord.

I do not want to upset them. I do not want them to stop being my friends by telling the truth. We cannot be friends with this world and friends with God. There is a direct contrast of this world and the things of God. We have to choose whose side we want to walk and remain on. How much are you willing to give up to remain friends with people who are seeking the same thing you are seeking, which is rest for their souls and eternal life?

Proverbs 18:24 *A man that hath friends must shew himself friendly: and there is a friend that sticketh closer than a brother.*

Does anybody know anybody that is not friendly

but expect everyone else to follow the rules of the Bible? All of us will experience this one time or another, but the truth of the matter is that the person that is not acting according to Word is not your example. We cannot control people, we are only accountable for our own actions, and we have an advocate which is the Father when we fall short of God's expectations of us.

Proverbs 19:4 *Wealth maketh many friends; but the poor is separated from his neighbor.*

Money will draw people from all walks of life into our lives. We have to be led by the Spirit of God when we are dealing with certain people. We all have family and friends that we want to help, but please do not take away the process for them. Sometimes we go through things so that God can work something out of us that should not be in us. Even for the ones we love so dearly, even the more, let us hear what the Father is saying.

We have to look at our situation and understand why we are friends with certain people and not friends with others. Could it be that the ones we are friends with are seeking the same thing or do we recognize that what is in them is also in us? That is why we need our Spirit operating so we can hear what the Father is saying to us, the church and about us, regarding the church. Our perception of people also causes us to accept or reject a person in the natural and the Spirit.

Luke 16:9 *And I say unto you, Make to yourselves friends of the mammon of unrighteousness; that, when ye fail, they may receive you into everlasting habitations.*

We have to be careful who we become friends with because some people are miserable and they want others with them who can share in the misery. Anybody remember a situation where you were trying to help your friend and you knew you were doing the wrong thing? Do you remember how your friend reacted because you told your friend the right thing? How did you feel after your friend reacted in such a negative way? We cannot make anyone do anything; we have to let them know what the Word of God says and be there if they need help. God allows someone to do the same thing for us. *I AM SCREAMING, CAN YOU HEAR ME?*

ADDITIONAL SCRIPTURES:
Proverbs 19:4
John 15:13
Proverbs 18:24
Proverbs 14:20
Luke 12:4

I AM SCREAMING BECAUSE I am born into privilege; I did not know I needed Jesus. I do not know what to do. Why do I need somebody when I have everything?

Genesis 2:7 says: *And the Lord God formed man of the dust of the ground, and breathed into his nostrils the breath of life; and man became a living soul.*

We have to know that God is the Supreme Being, and that we do not know more than God does. We have to make a decision regarding accepting Jesus Christ as our personal Savior because no one can make that decision for us. This is an individual walk, and when we stand before the judgement; we have to stand before God for ourselves. God really loves us to give His only begotten son for a dying world. Why would God who does not care send His only son to die, give us instructions (through the Word of God) and provided us with the Holy Spirit which guides us unto all truths?

Psalm 22:29 says: *All they that be fat upon earth shall eat and worship: all they that go down to the dust shall bow before him: and none can keep alive his own soul.*

Psalm 103:14 says: *For he knoweth our frame; he remembereth that we are dust.*

The Word of God reminds us that everything was put here on earth for us to enjoy. However, the things on earth should not take the place of God in our lives. We should worship the Lord and Him only should we serve. But we all know that people can get caught up in their houses, children, jobs, and other material possessions that focus on more than the Lover of our souls. This bring to mind a sermon Bishop Davis preached about inner vows. The message talked about how we make vows in our hearts because of things we feel may have been missing as we were growing up. Bishop Davis, reminded us that we never took the time to ask God about certain things; instead we made vows out of our emotions.

John 6:65 says: *And he said, therefore said I unto you, that no man can come unto me, except it were given unto him of my Father.*

John 14:6 says: *Jesus saith unto him, I am the way, the truth, and the life: no man cometh unto the Father, but by me.*

Genesis 2:7 says: *And the Lord God formed man of the dust of the ground, and breathed into his nostrils the breath of life; and man became a living soul.*

How can we believe that God does not know our Spirits when He is the one who created us? He already knows who will accept Him. We cannot even come to the Father unless we are drawn by the Holy Spirit.

John 12:40 says: *The enemy has blinded their minds and deadened their hearts so they can neither see with their eyes nor* *understand with their neither hearts nor turn—and I would heal them.*

Proverbs 14:12 says: *There is a way which seemeth right unto a man, but the end thereof are the ways of death.*

The enemy/devil is on his job and is fighting us from birth so we do not come into the knowledge of God and walk in our destiny. Most of the time we do not even realize that the enemy is fighting us, and just because we are not aware does not make him (the enemy) stop fighting us. We cannot afford to focus on our perception of things because we are dealing with a great deliverer. Focusing on what Word of God says does not have anything to do with how we feel, how we perceive things, but it is truly about the instructions from the Word of God. The Bible says that Jesus is the same yesterday, today and forever.

MIND

I AM SCREAMING BECAUSE I have finally got what the Word of God is saying to me and I am trying to reach my brother.

Let us remember that God came to deliver us from somewhere and something. Some people like where they are and you cannot make them change, you just have to give them the Word and let them choose righteousness just like you did.

Matthew 10:14 says: *And whosoever shall not receive you, nor hear your words, when ye depart out of that house or city, shake off the dust of your feet.*

some people once they finally receive Christ, forget about the love and compassion that Jesus Christ first drew them with. They just want to beat Jesus over the people head, and that is not the way we win people to Christ.

The Scripture says, "*With loving kindness have I drawn thee.*" We have to understand that God really does have our best interest in mind when He created the world, man, and gave instructions through the Word of God for our fulfilled life. Just because (we) people do not believe in God does not take away any of His power, omnipresence, presence or cause for Him to change His mind about us.

Proverbs 14:12 says: There is a way which seemeth right unto a man, but the end thereof are the ways of death.

We do not realize that something is missing until we try to fill the void in our heart with everything we can think of and nothing make us feel better. We have to lead people to their own discoveries. This means that we need to minister by the leading of the Holy Ghost so people will be convinced for themselves that they need Jesus, and without Him they will go to Hell. Some of us felt we were right and did not see anything wrong with the way we were living until someone told us from the Word of God our fate, if we continue on the path we were traveling on.

Psalm 16:11 says: *Thou wilt shew me the path of life: in thy presence is fullness of joy; at thy right hand there are pleasures for evermore.*

I love this Scripture because whenever there is something too big or too much for me, my Father is always by my side to create a way of escape. There is life in the Word of God and we have to search the Scriptures to see what God says about any circumstance that we may face. One thing is for certain is that He loves us and He will never leave us nor forsake us. Choose Jesus and His righteousness and watch your own life transform into something beautiful and peaceful.

Psalm 61:3 says: *For thou hast been a shelter for me, and a strong tower from the enemy.*

Even in our shortcomings and frailty, He is still protecting us and loving, if we allow Him to. We have to accept Him into our hearts and every part of our lives.

Proverbs 19:21 says: *There are many devices in a man's heart; the counsel of the Lord, that shall stand.*

We have to know that our truths are not necessarily God's truths unless they come from the Word of God. God's way is the only way we will win every time and in every situation. Sometime we confine Him to our Spirits and He is concerned about every part of us not just our Spirit and our problems. He desires to commune with us.

Revelation 3:20 says: *Behold, I stand at the door, and knock: if any man hear my voice, and open the door, I will come in to him, and will sup with him, and he with me.*

He desires us and desires to lead us to all truth, but it is a true choice of the heart. He has the power to come in, but He does not use His power to come in. We have to invite Him into our hearts and lives. Will you let Him come in and make you over again? The Word of God says in

Jeremiah 29:11 says: *For I know the thoughts that I think toward you, saith the Lord, thoughts of peace, and not of evil, to give you an expected end.*

We have to remember that Jesus gave His son to save us. I do not think anyone of us would give our child for anyone, much less to die for anyone.

Ephesians 1:3 says: *Blessed be the God and Father of our Lord Jesus Christ, who hath blessed us with all Spiritual blessings in Heavenly places in Christ.*

There is not anything that I would stake my life on, but Jesus. I would stake my life, death and everything else on Him. Personally, one day I remember having dinner at the dinner table with my husband and children. (We realize that the dinner table has been the place of many teachable moments because our children seem to be very attentive and open). My husband was telling the children about his pivotal moment in his education. He had told them that his mom was constantly coming up to the school because he was always getting into trouble. He said that his mom sat him down and at that moment, he realized that he had to make a change. I gave my story, and everyone thought I was goody too shoes, and that was alright for me because I was who I was and I was not going to apologize about how God had saved me and delivered me from so many things in my life. I had stomach ulcers, stress, infidelity, etc. I had to hold on to every Word of God I had heard so much about throughout my life. The conversation gave me an epiphany which was at that time in our lives did not know Jesus as Lord and Savior of our lives, and if either of us had died in our sinful state, hell was going to be where we spent eternity. Sometimes we feel like we have done so much so

God will not forgive us. On the other hand, there are those of us who feel like we are alright because we have not smoked, drank, fornicated or did drugs, etc. In both of these scenarios, at that time in our lives neither of us knew Jesus as Lord and Savior and we both were headed to hell. Galatians 5:1 says: Stand fast therefore in the liberty wherewith Christ hath made us free, and be not entangled again with the yoke of bondage.

The point is, it does not matter what you or I have done or what we have not done; we all have to accept Jesus in our hearts as our Lord and Savior. Sometimes trying to understand instead of doing what the Word says will cause us to falter in our walk with our Personal Savior. There is so much liberty in Jesus, but when we choose to do things different, then we get off course and allow the enemy room in our lives. Being in the hand of the living God is awesome.

1 Corinthians 2:14 says: *But the natural man receiveth not the things of the Spirit of God: for they are foolishness unto him: neither can he know them, because they are Spiritually discerned.*

We do not need to understand everything that is going on in our lives, but we need to apply the principles of God by the direction of the Holy Spirit in our lives. Sometimes, we want to understand everything that is going on in our lives, and I know because I was one of those people. I was so analytical about most things in my life and I worked hard to put my life the way I wanted it to be. Even though I knew what the Word say, it was a constant battle between my Spirit and my mind. I had to cultivate my relationship with Jesus so that I could become and stay consistent.

Deuteronomy 30:19 says: *I call Heaven and earth to record this day against you, that I have set before you life and death, blessing and cursing: therefore choose life that both thou and thy seed may live:*

This is truly our own choice, but we all should thank God for the opportunity to come into the knowledge of Jesus Christ because the Scripture tells us that all of us will not make it into Heaven. The Word of God says that judgement will begin at the house of the Lord, where will the ungodly and sinners appear? This tells me to be real and seek God not my own feelings and what I think about things. I had to change "my mindset" so I could renew my life. Oh what a blessing He has favored me with. It does not matter what the world do, we have to hold true to the one who can deliver our soul to hell, Jesus.

ADDITIONAL SCRIPTURES:
Ephesian 4:1-2
Psalm 15:1-2
2 Corinthians 7:1

Dr. M. H. Hancock

Isaiah 33:15-16
Psalm 101:6
1 Thessalonians 2:19

SUMMARY

We have the keys to the "game of life" through the Word of God and yet the enemy, self, and other obstacles causes us to doubt our Heavenly Father in so many situations. Personally, in my life, I got to a point that I became tired of going in circles, experiencing the same defeats over and over again. I had to bring attention to my relationship with Christ my Savior, so I might become more personal. I knew God had a plan for my life, but I had to figure out how to consistently allow Him to rule so I could win in every situation.

Please understand, winning doesn't always mean things will be comfortable. Number one the Scripture says *God chastens the ones He loves.*

Hebrews 12:10-11 says: *They disciplined us for a little while as they thought best; but God disciplines us for our good, in order that we may share in his holiness. [11]No discipline seems pleasant at the time, but painful. Later on, however, it produces a harvest of righteousness and peace for those who have been trained by it.*

It just means, I am going to trust Him at His Word. Then and only then did I start to see God's plans for my life unfolding. There are going to be heart aches such as death, disappointment, challenges and obstacles will challenge our believing what the Word of God is saying. We really are Spiritual beings living in the carnal world, and as we begin to develop and nourish our relationship with Jesus, we will see our whole world change because we have changed. It does not matter what has happened since you have accepted Christ, every day is filled with new mercies. We all get a chance to start over because of His grace and mercies. Experiencing pain, disappointments, and constant state of failure in one's own eyes can cause a shift in focus. This is why it is important for us to remember to whom everything belong and realize we are managers of the things God has given us. Once we realize God is in control of everything and He is expecting us to operate within the realms of the Word of God. Sometimes we do not understand why our finance is not working for us when we are tithing and giving offerings, but our life living does not reflect "what we know" and what the Word of God says. Sometimes we think God is just controlling our Spirits and not any other part of our lives. The quicker we can align our minds, our lives, and our wills to THE WILL of God, we will stop stressing ourselves out and realize that we move, exist and having our being BECAUSE of who we are and whose we are, Jesus's. There was a lesson on Stewardship and for me that solidified some things in my life. God is the OWNER of everything and we are the MANAGERS, and one day He is coming back and we have to give an account of our efforts, talents, time and money.

ABOUT THE AUTHOR

Dr. Hancock is a resident of Columbia, SC with husband of 25 years. They have three lovely daughters. Dr. Hancock is a graduate of the University of South Carolina with a doctorate degree in Curriculum and Instruction. Dr. Hancock is a thirteen year veteran educator.

Dr. Hancock's parents affirmed to all she and her 12 siblings that there is a higher authority, God and that everything and everyone has a purpose. She is a U.S. Army veteran. She fought in Operation Desert Storm in 1990. She is a freelance writer. She has a previous work published entitled **What to Do When: From Spiritual Fulfillment to Self-Fulfillment Nothing Missing.**

REFERENCES

King James Holy Bible, Holman Bible Publishers Nashville Tennessee, 1999
Life Application Study Bible, 1983
The Nelson Study Bible, (The New King James Version) Thomas Nelson Bibles, 1982
www.Bible.com
www.Biblegateway.com
www.BibleontheWeb.com
www.Biblestudytools.com
www.Changingminds.org
www.merriam-webster.com

www.ingramcontent.com/pod-product-compliance
Lightning Source LLC
Chambersburg PA
CBHW062111290426
44110CB00023B/2776